The
MIRACLE
of the
ILLUMINATION
of
ALL CONSCIENCES

THOMAS W. PETRISKO

St. Andrew's Productions

CONSECRATION

This book is consecrated to the *Eternal Father*. May His will, through the grace of the Illumination, be done.

Copyright © 2000 by Dr. Thomas W. Petrisko
All Rights Reserved
ISBN: 1-891903-25-X

St. Andrew's Productions
6111 Steubenville Pike
McKees Rocks, PA 15136

Toll-Free:	(888) 654-6279
Tel:	(412) 787-9735
Fax:	(412) 787-5204
Internet:	www.saintandrew.com
E-mail:	email@saintandrew.com

Scriptural quotations are take from The Holy Bible —RSV: Catholic Edition. Alternate translations from the Latin Vulgate Bible (Douay Rheims Version —DV) are indicated when used. Some of the Scriptural quotations from the New American Baible: St. Joseph Edition, The New American Bible— Fireside Family Edition 1984-1985, The Holy Bible—Douay Rheims Edition, The New American Bible— Red Letter Edition 1986.

Cover Photo: Polar Ring Galaxy NGC 4650A. Believed to be possibly the remnants of colossal collisions between two galaxies sometime in the distant past, probably at least 1 billion years ago. (This photo is not related to the contents of this book and is used with the permission of the Space Telescope Science Institute, Baltimore, MD.)

Printed in the United States of America

ACKNOWLEDGMENTS
AND DEDICATION

I wish to thank those most helpful to me during the writing of this book: Robert and Kim Petrisko, Dr. Frank Novasack, Fr. Richard Foley, Fr. William McCarthy, Michael Fontecchio, Amanda DeFazio, Carole McElwain, Carol Jean Speck, Joan Smith, Janet Nath, Jim Petrilena, John Haffert, Mrs. B. Laboissonniere Ph.d., and the prayer group at the Pittsburgh Center for Peace.

As always, my family perservered and supported me generously with this effort; my wife Emily, daughters Maria, Sarah, Natasha, Dominique and my son, Joshua. This book is dedicated to the five of them, and any other little angels yet to come. A special note of appreciation to my mother and father, Andrew and Mary Petrisko, and my uncle, Sam.

Maria

Sarah

Joshua

Natasha

Dominique

ABOUT THE AUTHOR

D r. Thomas W. Petrisko was the President of the Pittsburgh Center for Peace from 1990 to 1998 and he served as editor of the Center's seven "Special Edition" newspapers. These papers, primarily featuring the apparitions and revelations of the Virgin Mary, were published in many millions throughout the world. He is the author of **The Fatima Prophecies**, *At the Doorstep of the World;* **The Face of the Father**, *An Exclusive interview with Barbara Centilli Concerning Her Revelations and Visions of God the Father;* **Glory to the Father**, *A look at the Mystical Life of Georgette Faniel;* **For the Soul of the Family**; *The Story of the Apparitions of the Virgin Mary to Estela Ruiz,* **The Sorrow, the Sacrifice and the Triumph;** *The Visions, Apparitions and Prophecies of Christina Gallagher,* **Call of the Ages, The Prophecy of Daniel, In God's Hands;** *the Miraculous Story of Little Audrey Santo,* **Mother of The Secret, False Prophets of Today, St. Joseph and the Triumph of the Saints, The Last Crusade, The Kingdom of Our Father, Inside Heaven and Hell** and **Inside Purgatory**.

The decree of the Congregation for the Propagation of the Faith (AAS 58, 1186 - approved by Pope Paul VI on 14 October 1966) requires that the *Nihil obstat* and *Imprimatur* are no longer required for publications that deal with private revelations, apparitions, prophecies, miracles, etc., provided that nothing is said in contradiction of faith and morals.

The author hereby affirms his unconditional submission to whatever final judgment is delivered by the Church regarding some of the events currently under investigation in this book.

CONTENTS

*O*nce I was summoned to the judgment (seat) of God. I stood alone before the Lord. Jesus appeared such as we know Him during His Passion. After a moment, His wounds disappeared except for five, those in His hands, His feet and His side. Suddenly I saw the complete condition of my soul as God sees it. I could clearly see all that is displeasing to God. I did not know that even the smallest transgressions will have to be accounted for.

— Saint Faustina Kowalska

FOREWORD

THE ILLUMINATION
by Fr. Richard Foley, SJ

The amazingly prolific Dr. Thomas Petrisko here presents us with yet another searching and comprehensive study. His latest deals with an awesome impending event, that will be divine in origin and global in scope. Indeed, it is sure to make a mighty moral impact on the entire human race. For it will act on the conscience of each and every one of the six billion humans inhabiting planet earth.

This future event (many would say it is *near*-future) is variously referred to as the illumination of conscience, the mini-judgment, and the warning. And it will clearly come into our world as a super-grace, bringing multitudes of people much closer to the God of the ten commandments than they were before.

How do we know about this apocalyptic event lying ahead of the human race? We do so on the testimony, the prophetic testimony, of many saints, mystics and visionaries over recent centuries. In their various ways they tell us that the conscience-stirring event will come as the result of God's intervention and as an expression of his tender mercy.

Dr. Petrisko clearly indicates the consensus among the numerous prophetic witnesses on the central fact that a penetrating light will enable each of us to see our inner world of conscience as it appears in God's sight.

Clearly this illumination will come as a very choice grace, a mega-grace. For it will act within our minds and hearts as a mini-judgment, practically a rehearsal for the real one immediately after death. Miraculously we shall see, in a flash and with blinding clarity, the whole story of our lives; our moral track-record to date.

Doubtless the experience will come as something of a shock for everyone, not least heavy and habitual sinners. For all will perceive, intimately and contritely, what an evil thing sin is in itself, being an abomination that defiles the sinner because it defies and offends the all-holy Creator, the God of eternal rewards and punishments.

In addition we shall see in our illuminated consciences the multitudinous sins of thought, word, deed and omission that litter our past lives. And no doubt we shall want to identify with Cardinal Newman's great confession of sinfulness: "What is my life, dear Lord, but one series of offences, little and great, against thee?"

What emerges very prominetly from this book is the vital role played by conscience in the drama of every human life. It is that apparatus, so to call it, whose functioning enables us to evaluate our thoughts, words, deeds and omissions in terms of the ten commandments and the Church's general teaching.

The author also deals very finely and firmly with the subject of God's eventual judgment on our moral performance during life; in other words, how we have cooperated with the dictates of conscience within us.

Another feature of this remarkable book is that it presents us with the prophetic and convergent testimonies of such a large and wide variety of saints, mystics and visionaries over the past centuries.

Any number of illustrious names feature in this line-up. For example, St Edmund Campion in the 16th century joins prophetic hands with Blessed Anna Maria Taigi and St. John Vianney in the 19th. As for the 20th century, it abounded in witnesses to the coming miraculous illumination; they include several visionaries as well as mystics such as Teresa Neumann. At the present time, Fr. Stefano Gobbi and Barbara Centilli are among those who echo the selfsame prophetic message as did their predecessors.

Finally, the miraculous illumination, to quote a well-known contemporary, Maria Esperanza of Betania, will be primarily the occasion and cause of much joy--joy in the Lord of conscience. And she further speaks for all her fellow-witnesses when she affirms that the coming event will usher in a new era of universal holiness and peace.

Fr. Richard Foley, SJ
April 28, 2000
Easter Friday

The Last Judgment by Michaelangelo

INTRODUCTION

"An end is coming, the end is coming upon you! See it coming! The climax has come for you who dwell in the land! The time has come, near is the day; a time of consternation, not of rejoicing ...I will judge you according to your conduct and lay upon you the consequences of your abominations."

— **Ez 7:7**

According to the Jewish, Christian, and Muslim faiths, at death every soul must stand before the judgment seat of God to be accused, examined, and then sentenced. Known as the "Particular Judgment" to Christians, this moment is experienced as God's loving embrace for those who have been faithful, one in which the justified soul is welcomed into an eternity of bliss. However, for the unrepentant, it is a moment of terror when the sinner's conscience is said to be pierced with such a penetrating light of truth that eternal damnation becomes a self-inflicted sentence. At that point, as Pope John Paul II asserts in his 1999 catechesis on Hell, Divine Justice needs only to "ratify" the soul's decision.

Whether or not we are found worthy of Heaven or deserving of Hell, all of us must submit to judgment. Theologians believe it is an experience that intellectually "illuminates" our soul, allowing us to have complete awareness of our entire past in a glance, while simultaneously showing us how God judged each decision and choice in our life in accordance with His Divine Will. Theologians also tell us that before the judgment seat of God, our life is subjected to the most rigid moral and spiritual scrutiny, as our memory and conscience, in the light of God, provides us not only with an account of our sins but also our thoughts, words, desires, deeds, and omissions—both good and bad. Consequently, the piercing light of God's truth is said to leave nothing hidden or concealed, nothing to be falsely perceived or unjustly rationalized.

Thus, as theologian Fr. Federico Suarez writes, the soul is left with the consequence of subtracting "what has been of it's life from what ought to have been." With masks removed and disguises abandoned, says Fr. Suarez, "each one will be seen in the reality of God's truth. For he reminds us, "each man will face God alone, and each will be personally answerable for his own life."

But before this decisive moment of total moral awareness can occur, we must first undergo death. For only death can trigger this process of judgment.

Analogies between divine and human justice might highlight the similarities, but they must also include the obvious differences. Divine Justice is perfect; human justice is not. And despite our human attempt to understand Divine Justice, man—with few exceptions—has never known it in this life. Until our Particular Judgment, we are not able to see ourselves as God does, especially with all our faults and sins.

But what if God allowed us to undergo the "experience" of Particular Judgment before our actual death? Would it help us change "now" before we died? What if "all" of us could see ourselves in the clarity of divine justice, if only for a few moments? What if all earthly humanity simultaneously experienced such "reality"? Would the world suddenly change for the better?

For several hundred years, a prophecy has circulated among Christians foretelling a day of divine justice—a unique day, a day that would bring immediate and miraculous change in the world.

But this prophetic day of justice, unlike others describing God's angry wrath, is to be a day reportedly ordained by God as a "gift" to His people.   This gift would allow us to see ourselves and our lives through God's eyes now—before our death.

The prophets say that this will be a day of judgment for the "entire" world. But unlike the day of judgment at the end of our life, and the General Judgment at the end of the world, this miraculous "day of judgment" is to be given to mankind now, during this epoch in history. It is to be given, visionaries say, as an opportunity for countless souls to change for the better and return to God. It is also being given as an opportunity for the world, as a whole, to turn away from it's evil path and back towards its Creator. And finally, it is to be given to the world not just as invitation for people and the world to change, but especially as a chance for hardened sinners, individuals who otherwise would never repent, to save their souls from eternal damnation.

Known by various names— the "illumination of conscience," the "warning," the "judgment in miniature,"and more—this long foretold miracle is supposed to be a global event occurring in a flash of time, leaving the world changed, never to be the same again. It is an event some writers say is cryptically alluded to in both the Old and New Testaments. Most of all, as John Haffert, the founder of the Blue Army explains in his book, *The Great Event,* it is to be a "great event."

How will this "great event"occur? How will something this extraordinary really happen? According to visionaries, the divine will of God has ordained it and it will occur through His granting of a great, singular grace to the world. Accordingly, through this grace, the conscience of every one of us—man, woman, and child—will be supernaturally illuminated by God's divine truth, allowing us to see ourselves through the eyes of God. It will be an experience, the prophets say, similar to the Personal or Particular

Judgment at the time of death—one in which we will instantaneously see all our past sins as God sees them and know, without a doubt, that God "exists." Most importantly, after our experience with divine truth, we will realize that God's forgiveness and helping hand is waiting for us. And that all we need to do is ask.

According to God's chosen ones over the centuries, especially a number of prophetic voices in the past two decades, this worldwide illumination of all consciences will occur soon and will serve as a "correction" in the history of man. Having deviated from our true course, it will "reorient" us on our salvation journey, "redirecting us back toward our intended goal— reunion with our God, our Creator, our Father.

In reorienting mankind, this foretold miracle will inaugurate a new era on earth, a period foretold in Scripture: people will lay down their anger, along with their weapons, and spiritually return home to their Heavenly Father's love and protection. According to the prophets, as the doors of hearts and consciences open, as people see themselves in the burning fire of divine truth, this "judgment in miniature" will bring, after the period of purification which is to follow the illumination, the long prophesied triumph of the Church on earth, the awaited Era of Peace promised by the Virgin Mary in her 1917 apparitions at Fatima, Portugal.

Over the years, writers have attempted to establish and interpret the principal elements of this approaching day. They have theorized how this "judgement" will actually occur on earth. They have also proposed its individual and collective effects. This account will seek to do the same. We will not only explore what has been revealed about this foretold miracle, but also what we can do— before and after it occurs.

But to truly understand the significance of this prophecy, we should first understand exactly how our conscience functions, how God uses the conscience at the Personal and General Judgements to permit souls to "judge" themselves, and how it will be through God's love for His children, His burning desire to save their souls, that He will grant the world an illumination of its conscience. Thus, with such an understanding, we will then be able to look more profoundly at the miracle itself, and to hopefully come to realize why it will be the ultimate fulfillment of God's promise of "Divine Mercy" in our time.

"This is what God expects from us. He expects us to be sure to the best of our ability that our conscience is accurate and that we realize our obligations to make moral judgements in accordance with absolute truth."

CHAPTER ONE

THE FUNCTION OF CONSCIENCE

"By your words you will be acquitted and by your words you will be condemned."

— Mt 12:37

Ultimately, our eternal destiny — be it Heaven or Hell — is determined by whether or not we act honestly in accordance with the dictates of our conscience. According to traditional Catholic teaching, there are three primary elements that form what we call *conscience*:

1) What we know to be right, the innate moral knowledge of right and wrong in our mind, through the use of our unaided ability to reason. We know from Scripture, science and experience that God has infused this ability into every soul.

2) What we have learned to be right or wrong from others, such as parents, teachers, priests, etc.

3) What we have learned to be right or wrong from our own behavior, from our own personal experiences in life—both good or bad.

Theologians tell us that these three elements, with the aid of the Holy Spirit, combine to form a working conscience, which is a function of our mind. Once we understand how each one works and how they work together, we can then understand why, at our judgement,

God holds us accountable for all of our deeds or omissions, and how a soul can condemn itself to Hell before Divine Justice. Let us briefly examine each element:

1) Theologians believe that since we are made in the image of God, God instilled within us a capacity to have knowledge of things that is amazingly accurate and complete. This is confirmable in many ways, as even scientific studies reveal how humans understand the truth of things, without any education, but through reason. Moreover, this built-in insight cannot be lied to. We often know the truth without knowing "how" we know it. We constantly look at and evaluate things and then pass judgement. This internal process of insight, evaluation, and judgment is, therefore, complete without any necessary knowledge. Thus, each insight of the mind is an act of the mind to attempt to determine truth, and once the truth is determined, we cannot lie to ourselves about it, although we can and do change or override it. The way we do this often involves the second element of our conscience.

2) In addition to an innate knowledge of truth, we also derive truth from formal education. We learn from books, teachers, school, the experiences of others, etc. From childhood on, we are always discovering truth this way. Our minds, once again, accept these truths through the same process of insight, explanation and judgement. Together with our ability to "know" truth, our minds establish principles of truths that are known to be accurate and trustworthy, and thus, our conscience is further formed.

3) The third element of conscience formation comes from our experiences. From our own moral or immoral behavior, we experience subjective and objective truths. From these experiences, we often learn either good effects or bad

consequences, and we make decisions as to whether or not we want to conform to the good or to accept the bad, and whether or not to repeat such choices. And since we all have been given free will, we can choose to do the latter— we can choose to do bad, to repeatedly sin, for despite our consciences, we are still under no obligation to do what is right.

Now in order to please God by refraining from sin, we must always strive to act with at least a subjectively "certain" conscience. This means we should be honest with ourselves and want to know the truth in all matters. Christians must "want to avoid sin." This is what God expects from us. He expects us to be sure to the best of our ability that our conscience is accurate and that we realize our obligations to make moral judgements are in accordance with absolute truth.

God has created our minds to desire the truth, to discover it with effort, but when we attempt to lie to ourselves, when we attempt to say sin is not sin, God has given us a built-in process that detects and registers deliberate error. This process is called "guilt." Moreover, when we deliberately override our consciences repeatedly, we allow sin to dampen or blunt the sensitivity of our conscience, this in turn leads to a blindness of sin, a callousness towards its seriousness. It is what St. Paul meant when he said; "God delivered then up to a reprobate sense" (Rom 1:28).

However, if we lead a virtuous life by praying for and working to find the truth by constantly striving to conform to our conscience, acting with a "certain" conscience, then we live in truth. And the consequences of living in truth are rewarding. For the most part, we are happy, joyful, and at peace. We become free—free of anxieties, guilt, and doubt. Jesus promised that "if you continue in my word, you shall be my disciples indeed. And you shall know the truth, and the truth shall make you free" (Jn 8:31-32). Most importantly, we are free to live without fear of death and damnation. For on our day of judgment, we can then be reasonably "certain," rather than shocked or surprised, by God's justice.

"The Father has given over to him power to pass judgment because he is Son of Man; No need for you to be surprised at this, for an hour is coming in which all those in their tombs shall hear his voice and come forth. Those who have done right shall rise to live; the evildoers shall rise to be damned. I cannot do anything of myself, I judge as I hear, and my judgment is honest because I am not seeking my own will but the will of him who sent me."

-Jn 5:28-30

CHAPTER TWO

THE PARTICULAR JUDGMENT

"And as it is appointed unto men once to die, and after this, the judgment."

— Heb 9:27

JN 5-19:30

Isolemnly assure you, the son cannot do anything by himself—he can do only what he sees the Father doing. For whatever the Father does, the Son does likewise.

For the Father loves the Son and everything the Father does he shows him. Yes, to your great wonderment, he will show him even greater works than these.

Indeed, just as the Father raises the dead and grants life, so the Son grants life to those to whom he wishes,

The Father himself judges no one, but has assigned all judgment to the Son,

So that all men may honor the Son just as they honor the Father. He who refuses to honor the Son refuses to honor the Father who sent him.

I solemnly assure you, the man who hears my word and has faith in him who sent me possesses eternal life. He does not *come under condemnation, but has passed from death to life.*

I solemnly assure you, an hour is coming, has indeed come, when the dead shall hear the voice of the Son of God, and those who have heeded it shall live.

Indeed, just as the Father possesses life in himself, so has he granted it to the Son to have life in himself.

The Father has given over to him power to pass judgment because he is Son of Man;

No need for you to be surprised at this, for an hour is coming in which all those in their tombs shall hear his voice and come forth.

Those who have done right shall rise to live; the evildoers shall rise to be damned.

I cannot do anything of myself, I judge as I hear, and my judgment is honest because I am not seeking my own will but the will of him who sent me.

*

Before going any further, we need to make clear that on "two" different occasions, every soul will appear in the presence of the Lord to render an account of all of one's words, thoughts, and actions and to receive a sentence from Divine Justice. Simply stated, each soul will experience two "judgment days." The first judgment is called the "Particular Judgment" and occurs instantly at death. The second judgment will occur at the end of the world, when every soul shall stand together before the Lord, at what is known as the "General Judgment" of all mankind. This is the universal judgment where every soul's life will be made publicly manifest before all and eternal sentences received. Scripture indicates that this judgment will judge history, the good and evil works of not just souls, but cities, nations, tribes, and even "generations" of people.

THE PARTICULAR JUDGMENT

According to Tradition, the Particular Judgment of a soul takes place at the very moment a person dies, and perhaps, according to Doctor of the Church, St. Alphonsus Liguori, in the very place where the soul is separated from the body. Jesus Christ Himself, Tradition holds, comes to judge "at that hour you think not the Son of Man will come" (Luke 12:40). "For the just, He will come in love," writes St. Augustine, "for the wicked in terror."

Theologians tell us the Particular Judgment is instantaneous. During this experience, the soul is enlightened in a decisive and inevitable way about all its merits and failings. It sees the evil of its life, it's omissions, how it failed in its vocation, and it's conscience is penetrated by this profound reality. According to the acclaimed theologian Fr. Garrigou Lagrange, the announcement of the sentence is also instantaneous. It is rendered not by a voice, but in a spiritual way, so that a soul awakens to all its errors, sees how God has judged them, and in it's conscience, accepts the correctness of the judgment. Therefore, says Fr. Lagrange, it is true to say that a person is truly "*judged.*" Fr. Lagrange asserts that the sentence is immediate, as there is nothing to retard it. Whether to Heaven, Hell or Purgatory, souls go without delay.

There are several aspects of the Particular Judgment worth noting. At this judgment, a soul sees God only intuitively, otherwise that soul would be beatified— which cannot take place until it is in Heaven. The Particular Judgment also assigns each soul their place in eternity, although the General Judgment still remains necessary. And finally, it is important to note that any soul sent to Purgatory is saved and will eventually be admitted to Heaven.

"The sins of the reprobate shall be seen by all at a glance, as in a picture."

\- St. Basil

Witnessing the Miracle of the Sun at Fatima, Oct. 13, 1917.

CHAPTER THREE

THE GENERAL JUDGMENT

"And the sea gave up the dead that were in it, and death and hell gave up their dead that were in them; and they were judged, every one according to their works. ...And whosoever was not found written in the book of life, was cast into the pool of fire."
—Rv 20: 14-15

While the Particular Judgment is very individual, with each person experiencing an account of his/her life, the General Judgment at the end of the world is both personal and social. For we all interact with the world, affecting it and other souls, positively and/or negatively.

Because of this truth, the General Judgment will unmask the history of the world, its philosophies of truth or error, and how the affects of men last for generations. The secrets of history will be revealed to all, as will the secret lives of individuals. This is because truth and justice must be vindicated, as the good, who in their earthly lives often lost their reputation or were defeated by the wicked, will now triumph. At the General Judgment, all hypocrisy will be uncovered, all vanity will be exposed, and the humble and the proud will be seen in their true light. The truth of every event and every life will be seen.

For the Particular Judgment, our own conscience convicts us. According to St. Alphonsus Liguori, the same rule applies to the General Judgment:

> But behold the Judgment now commences. The books are opened; that is, the conscience of each one: "The Judgement sat, and the books were opened"(Dan 7:10). "The witnesses against the reprobate shall be, first, the devils..." said St Augustine. "Most just judge, declare him to be ours, one who would not be thine." Secondly, one's own conscience will testify: "Their conscience being witness to them" (Rom. 2:15). Finally, the Judge Himself, who has been present at all the offences committed against Him, shall be a witness: "I am the Judge and the witness, saith the Lord. (Jer. 29:23)

In the opinion of scholars, at the General Judgment sins of the elect will not be manifested, but concealed. They note the words of David and St. Paul, "Blessed are they whose iniquities are forgiven, and who sins are covered. Blessed is the man whose sin the Lord does not record" (Psalm 31:1, Rom 4:7-8). On the other hand, writes St. Basil, "The sins of the reprobate shall be seen by all at a glance, as in a picture."

In our world today, many claim to live by their consciences while openly taking immoral positions. This occurs when people accept wrong principles on purpose, failing to accept grievous error, or sin. It occurs when people do not strive to be "certain" in their conscience And it occurs when "tolerance" of sin dictates an "anything is permissible" philosophy, without regard to the consequences. In our world today, moral matters are considered insignificant and their truth not important. Moreover, morality and ethics have been reduced to matters of personal perceptions. This is not new. Throughout history, Church and moral leaders of the world have often "warned" of such errors and their consequences. Nations and civilizations have fallen because of such thinking, as is demonstrated by history. But especially today, when the loss of our immortal soul as the ultimate consequence of betraying one's conscience is not accepted or believed by many, since the responsibility for acting in truth is seen as not being serious, many people continue to live, and often die, in "serious sin."

Around the world, the prophetic voices of almost of every Christian denomination, as well as other religions, are telling us that mankind is in great darkness and that the degree of "grievous" sin (known as "mortal sin" to Catholics) is now epidemic. Pagan worship, murder, deceit, birth control, theft, envy, abortion, materialism, homosexuality, atheism—and various other sins—are alive and well in the hearts of people everywhere. Moreover, much of mankind claims to believe that such "sin" is not really sin at all.

*

FATIMA

Since Fatima, the Virgin Mary has been revealing in her apparitions that the world is more sinful than ever, more sinful and more atheistic, she says, than at the time of the great flood. Truth today is so lost, Mary reveals, that the most essential values of life are gone, totally discarded. Thus, the legal breakdown of the family, the cornerstone of civilization, is at stake for the first time in history. And because of this, the visionaries tell us that we are pushing the world to the brink of a cataclysmic event.

Indeed, wherever sin darkens the mind, danger exists. And now, the entire world faces the consequences of hatred, and atheism, mixed together with modern science (when it rejects God), and a Pandora's box of ungodly weapons of mass destruction. Powerful world leaders with little regard for absolute truths have forced the world into a dangerous balancing act of controlled madness. This danger is cumulative, progressive, and volatile. This "warning" was the principal theme of the Virgin Mary's Fatima message in 1917. It is also the message emanating from the Virgin Mary in her numerous apparitions since Fatima. And it is the force behind the plea of Pope John Paul II, whose appeals are always motivated by his unique insight into "the urgency" of our times.

For some time, the promise of a great miracle of mercy, a miracle of God's "divine mercy" has been foretold. It is to be a miracle of truth—one designed to hopefully move consciences in the direction of moral certainty, one designed to bring the world out of its darkness and closer to God. It is to be a miracle of "judgement"—one that will bring mankind so close to God, so close to His truth, that we will at first tremble in fear. But after the miracle is experienced and, hopefully, understood properly, people will abandon their fear and race into the arms of their God, Who desires to come closer to His children in this time—to save their souls and protect the world from total "annihilation."

The crowd at Fatima, Oct. 13, 1917, observing the Miracle of the Sun. Was this a foreshadowing of the Illumination?

CHAPTER FOUR

THE MIRACLE OF THE ILLUMINATION OF ALL CONSCIENCES

"I will bring your conduct down upon you; and the consequences of your abominations shall be in your midst: then you shall know that I am the Lord."

— Ez 7:4

I pronounced a great day, not wherein any temporal potentate should minister, but wherein the Terrible Judge should reveal all men's consciences and try every man of each kind of religion. This is the day of change.... — *St. Edmund Campion*

Whether St. Edmund Campion was speaking of the foretold miracle of the illumination of conscience is uncertain, but his words appear to be of a prophetic quality with regards to the great miracle that is now said to be very near. The prophecy of St. Campion is probably the oldest, most specific prophecy attributable to the miracle of the illumination of conscience. Saint Campion was born in London in the year 1540 and died as a martyr for the faith in 1581. He was canonized by Pope Paul VI in 1970 and reportedly received apparitions of the Virgin Mary. Moreover, St. Campion's words, are quite consistent with latter-day prophecies of an illumination of consciences:

1) The event will affect the consciences of all people, confronting truth within each soul.

2)   The event will effect every human being on earth, with no exceptions for believers or non-believers, Christians and non Christians.

3)   It will be an act of God's mercy, which will also resonate in souls as His justice.

4)   It will be a "Judgement" of the whole world, often referred to as a "Judgement in Miniature" by visionaries.

*

Over the centuries, certain "defining" words have been used to help describe this prophesied miracle. The most repeated terms are "great light," "reconciliation," "conscience," "restoration," "illumination," "enlightenment," "small last judgment," "the awakening" "the fearful moment," "day of the Lord," "mini-judgment," "day of light," "reckoning," "correction," "transformation," "judgment in miniature" and the " warning."

*

FACTS ABOUT THE ILLUMINATION

Since an event of this nature has never before occurred, and since no one has ever returned from the grave to describe their Particular Judgment, the specific details of this worldwide miracle of conscience cannot be fully explained, yet alone understood. And regardless of the prophetic source, this event will never be completely comprehended, not only before it occurs, but even after. Too many mysteries and variables are involved in this miracle, particulars only God comprehends and reserves for Himself. But from what we know about the function of conscience, what part it plays in the Particular and General Judgments, and what has been revealed about the coming miracle of the illumination of all consciences, we can paint a picture, although subjective, as to the event's general elements and how they will function collectively in its unfolding. And to a certain degree, the event's after-effects:

1) As a culmination of the intercessory efforts of the Virgin Mary over the past several centuries, and as a result of the prayers and sacrifices instigated through her extraordinary effort (such as the Five First Saturdays Devotion requested at Fatima), God has willed the great gift of renewal for the world. Therefore, the Second Pentecost will be like a heavenly dew of grace and of fire which will renew the whole world. The result of this action of divine love will be to bring the Church and the world into a new era of truth, holiness, love, justice, and peace. But before all this can occur, the door of each heart must be opened, the conscience of each soul must be illuminated— this is what the great miracle will do.

2) From a spiritual standpoint, the miracle of the illumination of all consciences will be a direct result of the coming of the Holy Spirit upon the earth, as He came upon the Apostles at Pentecost. This time, in the form of a "Second Pentecost," He will be coming upon the Church, and to a great degree, the entire world.

3) Each soul, during the moments of the illumination, will see his own life and all he has done in the very light of God. As if by a keen sword of divine truth, hearts and souls will be pierced. People will see themselves, as if standing before a mirror of truth or looking at an X-ray of their soul.

4) This miracle of the illumination of all consciences, which will allow people to see themselves in the burning fire of divine truth, will be like a presage of their "Particular Judgment." And because every soul in the world will simultaneously experience the illumination, it will serve as a "Judgment in Miniature" for the entire world.

5) This Mini-Judgment will serve as a purification of sin. After seeing our souls in the truth of God, many of us will be transformed by grace and holiness. The visionaries say that God desires that they hasten to Him for forgiveness. (It has been prophesied that priests and pastors and all religious figures will find it difficult to keep up with the many, who will flock to them to seek their help.)

6) The miracle of conscience will come directly from God and will be worldwide.

7) The illumination will be "seen" and "felt."

8) The miracle will be experienced everywhere at the same time.

9) Many people will feel "fear" from the illumination; some could die from this fear.

10) The experience of the miracle of conscience will apparently "coincide" with some visible "event in the sky," perhaps cosmic. (Some visionaries believe that an asteroid, comet, or some similar celestial object or objects will come close to the earth, perhaps even colliding with another such object or one another. This then will fulfill the element of the prophecy concerning a physical event that will be a visible manifestation or happening in the sky.)

11) Because a visible event is to deliberately coincide (see 10) with the unfolding of the miracle, some will "rationalize" the "illumination" and deny its truth. Subsequently, the proper response will be lost. But God has ordained this "visible" element of the miracle so this great event is still experienced and then accepted in "faith." Like all miracles, it is not going to be "provable" beyond a doubt that it came from God. One must still "believe" in what they experienced.

12) Each person will have a different degree of response to the awakening.

13) The miracle cannot be prevented.

14) For the very sinful, the illumination of conscience will appear to be a punishment.

15) For the just, the miracle will draw them closer to God.

16) The miracle will last only "a short time."

17) From the miracle, souls, even atheists, will know God exists, although they can reject or override this knowledge.

18) Many souls will reject the illumination, and move even farther away from God.

19) The illumination is to be one of God's last warnings to the world before the end of time.

20) The illumination will, in essence, be a miracle of the heart— from God's heart to the hearts of His children.

HOW WILL SOULS CHANGE?

After the miracle of the illumination souls will reportedly change. But how are they to change? According to what has been revealed, there are going to be three "primary" results, all of which are distinguishable:

1) Many souls, deep in sin, will experience strong, almost radical conversions to God. The illumination will leave them

humbled and compelled to change their lives. They will be appreciative, remorseful and eager to apply their "will" in the service of God. Some will answer their call, becoming great saints.

2) Some souls will regret and reject the grace of the illumination. Preferring to stay in sin, these individuals will turn away from God even more and fall deeper into sin. The contrast between the light and the darkness in the world will become greater because of these souls, for some will become "very dark". Such souls, like the souls in Hell, will oppose God even more and will only be able to be helped through intense prayer and sacrifice. It is important to note that these souls will not necessarily be the most hardened sinners. Rather, many will be the "lukewarm", who simply are not desirous of God's truth. They are the ones Christ says He will "spew out," souls enamored with the world and their lives, who, though not necessarily in the deepest sin, will prefer to hold onto their ways. God, unfortunately, will still not be of interest to them, even after their "warning."

3) For souls already in a state of grace, and who love God very much, there will come unique graces and blessings. These souls will be drawn extremely close to God and will come to know Him in a special way. After the illumination, they will burn with the fire of His divine love in their hearts and will come into close communion with Him. God will, in turn, subsume them into Himself. Their holiness will shine throughout the world and they will spread God's light and truth everywhere they go, bringing to reality the "era of peace" and the triumph of God in time and history.

CHAPTER FIVE

THE PROPHECIES

"These then are the things you should do: Speak the truth to one another; let there be honesty and peace in the judgment at your gate."

—Zech 8:16

In addition to St. Campion, other Catholic mystics from past centuries have referred to a coming illumination of conscience. Let us examine a few of these pre-20th century prophecies:

The Venerable Holzhauser (d. 1658):

The Hand of Almighty God will work a marvelous change, something apparently impossible according to human understanding.

Elizabeth Canori-Mora (d. 1825):

Then a "great light" appeared upon the earth which was the "sign of the reconciliation" of God with man.

Blessed Anna Maria Taigi, (d.1836):

A great purification will come upon the world preceded by an "illumination of conscience" in which everyone will see themselves as God sees them.

Prophecy of Mayence (d. 1854):

The good God shall save all. It will be like a sign of the Last Judgment.

Father Bernard Maria Clausi, O.F.M. (d. 1849)

Before the triumph of the Church comes, God will first take vengeance on the wicked, especially the godless. It will be a new "judgement," the like has never been seen before, and it will be universal.

Saint John Mary Vianney (d. 1859):

A time will come when people will believe that the end is near. It will be a sign of the Last Judgment.

Mari-Julie Jahenny (d. 1941):

One more judgment will take place before the last one, a judgment of justice...altogether with a judgment of glorious resurrection in peace and hope for the friends of God.

*

TWENTIETH CENTURY PROPHECIES

During the early part of the 20th century, the Bavarian stigmatist, Teresa Neumann, referring to a future time of warnings, said, "Our Lord Himself called it a '**Minor Judgment**.'" A decade or so later, noted Yugoslavian visionary, Julka, who was born in 1921, wrote that Jesus told her a **"small Last Judgment is approaching."**

In the 1940's, more visionaries throughout the world were speaking about the coming of a great miracle of conscience. In Heede, Germany, on November 1, 1937, four girls reported that the Blessed Virgin Mary, and later Jesus, appeared to them. The messages given to the girls, in a series of a hundred apparitions, were linked to Fatima. Again, strong reference was made to a coming "illumination of the minds of men." At Heede, Jesus reportedly explained to the children: **"I will come with My peace. With a few faithful, I will build up My Kingdom. As a flash of lightning this Kingdom will come....Much faster than mankind will realize. I will give them a special light. For some this light will be a blessing; for others, darkness. The light will come like the star that showed the way to wise men. Mankind will experience My love and My power. I will show them My justice and My mercy. My dearly beloved children, the hour comes closer and closer. Pray without ceasing!"** In another message given at Heede, Jesus told the four children, **"It will be terrible, a 'Minor Judgment.' I will make myself known to men. Every soul shall recognize me as their God."**

*

Christ's final words to the children at Heede, **"every soul shall know me as their God"** are perhaps most significant. For these words, unlike the literal interpretations of so many prophecies surrounding this event, give a more accurate understanding of how people should understand this miracle. Indeed, while fear and justice may be part of the unfolding of the miracle, in actuality, it will be a miracle of love more than anything else. God is going to come close to His children in a unique and special way, and though many will initially respond in fear, such is not God's intention or their need. This understanding will be developed later in the book.

Teresa Neumann   St. John Vianney   Mari-Julie Jahenny   Bl. Anna Maria Taigi

The reported visionaries at Garabandal

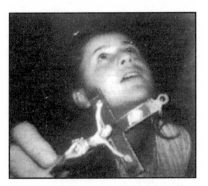

Conchita Gonzalaez in prayer

Conchita Gonzalez today

The reported visionaries at Garabandal

* Photographs courtesy of Mr. Stanley Karminski

CHAPTER SIX

GARABANDAL

"They shall come with fear at the thought of their sins, and their iniquities shall stand against them, to convict them."
— Wis 4:20

No apparition of the Virgin Mary is better known for the prophecy of the coming "illumination of conscience" than the reported apparitions at Garabandal, Spain, from 1961 through 1965. Although these apparitions have not yet been approved by the Church, they were not condemned and have had a vast, worldwide following over the years.

A reopening of the investigation in the late 1980's failed to produce any change in the Church's decision. In the past few years, the local bishop has asked the faithful to discontinue propagating the messages of Garabandal.

[Note: The account of the events at Garabandal given here acknowledges and complies to the bishop's authority and his wishes. The story of the reported events that occurred at Garabandal, as outlined in this chapter, is rendered in a journalistic, historical context which, as the great Mariologist Fr. Renee Laurentin asserts, is permissible. All authors, writers, journalists, etc., have the right to examine and report historical events, even when the Church issues a condemnation, which was not the verdict at Garabandal. Church scholars note that the historical record of any event, regardless of its determined merit, must always remain undistorted and uncensored, as long as there is also acknowledgment of the "determination" and/

or any recommendations from the local ordinary. As noted, the current bishop of Garabandal has discouraged propagation since the Church's investigation was unable to determine that the event was "supernatural." The Bishop of Santander's 1996 letter can be found at the end of this chapter.]

OVERVIEW OF THE EVENT

Four children in the village of Garabandal, Spain between 1960 and 1965 claimed the Virgin Mary appeared to them, beginning on June 18, 1961. Prophetic messages were reportedly given. Over the years, this apparition developed a great following of devoted believers. For our purposes, a promised worldwide "illumination" of the consciences of all people was prophesied by the Virgin Mary to precede (within twelve months) a great miracle foretold to occur at the site of the apparitions in Garabandal. The reports claim extraordinary mystical events such as Communion being given from the hands of angels and ecstasies involving contortions of the visionaries' necks, all witnessed and documented by film and still photography.

A retraction by one of the visionaries, Conchita Gonzalez, in addition to other questions, has made the situation surrounding the judgment of the apparitions very complex. Still, to this day, the devotees of Garabandal await the promised Warning (the illumination of all consciences), the Great Miracle and the Permanent Sign (to be also given at Garabandal). Reportedly all the sick present the day of the Great Miracle at Garabandal are promised to be "cured" and "unbelievers will be converted." One person, Father Luis Andrew a Jesuit seminary professor, was reportedly shown the miracle in a vision. On his return to the seminary, however, he died. The Church re-opened the investigation of Garabandal in the late 1980's.

THE ILLUMINATION OF CONSCIENCES PROPHECY

At Garabandal, the children reported that Mary spoke of an

approaching miracle that would involve a worldwide "illumination of consciences." It was known and referred to by the visionaries as the "Warning," reportedly because Mary herself used this term. (Note: This term for the miracle of the illumination of consciences, the "Warning," is recognized as having its origination from the reported apparitions of the Virgin Mary at Garabandal.)

According to the four children, the Great Miracle would occur in their "lifetimes," which if carried out to normal life expectancy, could be expected to occur sometime between now and the year 2025— although there have been subtle indications by some of the reported visionaries that this event is very near. The Illumination, according to the Garabandal visionaries, will supposedly be followed, within twelve months, by "the Great Miracle," another prophesied event revealed at Garabandal, and then by a purification, or chastisement. Let us now examine what each of the visionaries have stated for the record about the illumination over the last thirty years or more.

CONCHITA GONZALEZ

In a letter dated January 1, 1965, Conchita Gonzalez, one of the four visionaries at Garabandal, wrote: "Our Lady said that a 'warning' would be given to the entire world before the Miracle in order that the world might amend itself. It will come directly from God and be visible throughout the world." On June 2, 1965, Conchita wrote: "The Warning, like The Chastisement, is a fearful thing for the good as well as the wicked. It will draw us closer to God and warn the wicked that the end of time is coming. These are the last warnings."

In numerous accounts, Conchita has been quoted as saying that the illumination of all consciences will be a purification to prepare the world for the Miracle of Garabandal. And she believes that when these events occur we will be near the end of an era. According to Conchita, each person on earth will have this 'interior experience,' revealing how they stand in the light of God's justice. Believers and nonbelievers alike will experience the illumination. Not surprisingly, some have conjectured that the Miracle of the Sun at Fatima in 1917, which was none other than a ball of fire hurling toward the earth, was possibly a preview of this miracle. This is because it included a visible celestial object (like that which is to accompany the illumination) which induced a response from the people at Fatima, and because the event left people very changed. It also convinced them of the reality of God and of their own mortality. Russell Chandler, in his book *Doomsday* quotes Pope John XXIII as stating that the events at Fatima served as a connection to a possible future *"warning"* to the world, perhaps even the miracle of the illumination:

> Though Pope John XXIII did not reveal the Third Secret on schedule in 1960, he told a French philosopher and recorded in his journal that the fall of the sun at Fatima was more than a warning of possible nuclear war if society refused to change. 'It was eschatological,' he said, 'in the sense that it was like a repetition or an annunciation of a scene at the end of time for all humanity assembled together.'

Prior to the release of the Bishop's statement in 1996, author Michael Brown examined the events at Garabandal. The actual manifestation of the miracle of the illumination of all consciences, according to Brown, in *The Final Hour*, alludes to the occurrence of a simultaneous event in the sky, which Brown concluded from Conchita's words. Brown quotes Conchita words indicating some sort of tandem cosmic event:

> Like two stars...that crash and make a lot of noise, and a lot of light...but they don't fall. It's not going to hurt us but we're going to see our consciences. Although The Warning will not kill, some people may die from shock. When it comes, you will know we have opened up the end of time....the Virgin announced

this event by a word beginning with the letter "A"....it will be like a punishment, for the just and wicked alike. For the just, to bring them closer to God, and for the wicked, to announce to them that time is running out. Nobody could prevent The Warning from coming. It's a certainty, although I do not know the day or anything about the date.

Brown further stated in *The Final Hour*, that Conchita maintained that "the Warning will be visible throughout the entire world":

> In whatever place anyone might be....it will be like a revelation of our sins and it will be seen and experienced equally by believers and nonbelievers and people of any religion whatsoever. It will be like a purification before the miracle and "is a sort of catastrophe." It will make us think of the dead, that is, we would prefer to be dead than to experience The Warning. The Warning will not be explained by science but will be both seen and felt. The most important thing about that day is that everyone in the whole world will see a sign, a grace, or a punishment, within themselves. In other words, "a warning."

Father Joseph Pelletier also refers to what Conchita said in his book, *God Speaks At Garabandal*:

> I think that those who do not despair will experience great good from it [The Warning] for their sanctification.

According to Pelletier's account, Conchita told another interviewer in 1973,

> They [people] will find themselves all alone in the

world no matter where they are at the time, along with their conscience, right before God. They will then see their sins and what their sins have caused. We will all feel differently because it will depend on our conscience. The Warning will be very personal; therefore, we will all react differently to it. The most important thing will be to recognize our sins and the bad consequences of them. You will have a different view of The Warning than me because your sins are different than mine. The phenomenon will not cause physical damage, continued Conchita, but will horrify us because at that very moment we will see our souls and the harm we have done. It will be as though we were in agony but we will not die by its effects but perhaps we will die of fright or shock to see ourselves....No one will have doubts of it being from God, and of it not being human. We must always be prepared with our souls in peace and not tie ourselves down so much to this world.

In *Star On The Mountain*, by Father Mateine Laffineur, Conchita is further quoted as saying that the illumination will come "before the end of an era....which is not the end of the world itself."

MARI-LOLI MAZON

Mari-Loli Mazon, another visionary from Garabandal who now lives in Haverhill, Massachusetts, is the only Garabandal visionary who stated that she knew the year of the illumination. Says Loli, "We will see it and feel it within ourselves and it will be most clear that it comes from God." (Article by Mr. Stanly Karminski, Our Lady Queen of Peace, Special Edition II, Pittsburgh Center for Peace, December 1992.) Michael Brown writes in *The Final Hour* that Loli explains "everything will stand still for a few seconds—even planes in the sky." Loli adds, according to Brown's account, that it will seem as if, for a few moments, the "world is coming to a standstill," but so absorbing will be the experience that few will take note of their surroundings.

JACINTA GONZALEZ

Jacinta Gonzalez, a third Garabandal visionary, also describes the event:

> The Warning is something that is just seen in the air, everywhere in the world, and immediately is transmitted into the interior of our souls. It will last for a very little time, but it will seem a very long time because of its effect within us. It will be for the good of our souls, in order to see in ourselves, our conscience...the good that we have failed to do, and the bad we have done. Then we will feel a great love towards our heavenly parents and ask forgiveness for all our offenses. The Warning is for us to draw closer to Him and to increase our faith. Therefore, one should prepare for that day, but not await it with fear. God does not send things for the sake of fear but rather with Justice and love. He does it for the good of all His children so they might enjoy eternal happiness and not be lost.

According to Michael Brown's account in *The Final Hour*, Jacinta Gonzalez also states that she saw "prior to this event....a persecution or invasion by communists and was told to pray that this be avoided."

OTHER ACCOUNTS FROM GARABANDAL

In his book, *Garabandal: The Village Speaks*, author Ramon Perez reveals more about this great event:

> There will be a pre-warning before The Warning. The

pre-warning will be an event connected to the apparitions at Garabandal....at the Episcopal See of Santander, there will come a bishop who will not believe in these events at first. But the Blessed Virgin will give him a sign. He will then believe and will lift the prohibition for the priests to go to Garabandal. Conchita tells us the Warning will then be very close; the rest should not be long in coming. [This condition was reportedly fulfilled in the mid-1980's, although the apparitions were not approved.]

According to Perez's account, on September 13, 14, and October 22, 1965, Conchita gave precise details about the illumination of consciences:

If I did not know about the other chastisement to come, I would say there is no greater Chastisement than The Warning. Everybody will be afraid but Catholics will bear it with more resignation than others. It will last for only a short time. The Warning comes directly from God. It will be visible in every part of the world, no matter where we live! Oh yes! The Warning will be very formidable! A thousand times worse than earthquakes. It will be like fire; it will not burn our flesh but we will feel it corporeally and interiorly. All nations and every person on earth will feel it. No one shall escape it and unbelievers will feel the fear of God. One day, we are going to suffer a horrible catastrophe in all parts of the world. No one will escape it. It would be preferable to die than to bear for five minutes that which awaits us. We could suffer it in the day time as well as the night whether we are in bed or not!

Perez further reports that on August 15, 1972, Conchita warned of the consequences of rejection of the illumination of consciences:

The Warning....will not hurt the body. It will, however, cause us to suffer. Afterwards, if we do not change in spite of all these things [which are truly the last warnings, the last remedies that God will send us], He will send us a chastisement.

Several other interesting facts emerge from this account. Perez quotes an excerpt from a July 27, 1975 interview granted by Mari-Loli to Needles publication, now known as *Garabandal Magazine:*

Q.   How do you know that there will NOT be more than a year between the Warning(illumination) and the Miracle?

Loli: The Blessed Virgin told me during an apparition.

Q.   Are you afraid of The Warning?

Loli: Yes, like anyone else, I have faults and the Warning will make me see these faults, and that frightens me.

Q.   Can you tell us anything else about The Warning?

Loli: All I can say is that it is very near and that it is very important that we get ready for it, as it will be a terrible event. It will make us realize all the sins we have committed.

According to Perez's account, Mari-Loli also commented on the best place to be during the miracle:

I think the best place to be at the time is in church near the Blessed Sacrament. Jesus would give us the necessary strength to bear it. It will be a horror of the worst kind. If I could only tell you how the Virgin described it to me. But the Chastisement, that will be worse. We will understand that The Warning comes to us because of our sins. We cannot imagine how much we offend God. The Blessed Mother told me that people know very well there is a Heaven and a Hell. But can't we see that we think of it only through fear and not love of God? On account of our sins we have only ourselves to blame for The Warning. And we must suffer it for Jesus, for the offenses committed against God.

Robert Francois, in his book *Oh, Children Listen To Me: Our Lady Teaches at Garabandal*, adds additional insight to the illumination of all consciences. He reports that after the miracle, Conchita herself says "she would love God far more," and that in October, 1968, Conchita declared the prophesied illumination will be "a correction of the conscience of the world":

> In October 1968, Conchita declared that the prophesied Warning will be 'a correction of the conscience of the world.' Saint Paul tried 'to have a conscience clear of offense towards God or man, at all times' (Acts 23:1; 24:16) and he often urged his correspondents to live up to their conscience; for instance, when he wrote to the Christians of Rome to submit to the civil authorities 'for conscience's sake' (Rom. 13:5). Conscience is nothing else but human reason applied to the realm of morals. God has given it to us as a light to show us what is right and what is wrong.

Francois further comments on the unmistakable reality of this event:

> God's warnings are clear and unmistakable. He shows us through these marvelous events that it is really He who is talking to us. He has announced that

a great miracle will take place at Garabandal which, according to Conchita, will be a striking manifestation of His love. It will be preceded by a salutary warning of short duration to all mankind to make amends and benefit from the Miracle, thus avoiding the chastisement, conditional but fearful. The Warning will be perceived everywhere and by everyone. It will draw the good closer to God. The ugliness of our sins will be revealed. Unbelievers will feel the fear of God. It will be dreaded by all mankind. It will purify us and warn us of the Miracle to come which will take place not more than a year later. If we read carefully, we shall understand that the Warning is an extraordinary token of God's love.

Francois concludes that "this has already been said of the messages," and that "the Warning is meant to provoke our amendment, the amendment of many, perhaps all, as it will be seen and perceived in the whole world."

Author Judith Albright, in *Our Lady At Garabandal*, agrees. She writes, that according to Conchita, each person who experiences the illumination will have "a desire to amend one's life."

CONCLUSION

While the Church has ruled it could not find the events at Garabandal to be supernatural, the four reported visionaries' claims of being told by the Virgin Mary of the coming illumination has always and still inspires followers of the apparitions. This is because no one can explain how four very young uneducated peasant children from a remote mountainous village could, simultaneiously and individually, explain under intense cross examination the details of of a very extraordinary and unique prophecy. Undoubtedly, many hope the fulfillment of this miracle, the miracle of the illumination of all consciences, to be followed by the Great Miracle in the village within a year, will encourage the Church to reopen its investigation.

*

THE INSIGHT OF FATHER BEBIE

Father Phillip Bebie, C.P., whose book *The Warning* was written shortly before his death, wrote that no person can deny the great mercy the illumination of conscience will bring with it. According to Bebie, a soul's response should be one of gratitude and conversion. Father Bebie was considered an expert on this prophecy and his booklet was intended to be available and mass-produced immediately after the illumination was experienced:

> It will be an act of God...an act of His Mercy. Whether the world will avoid annihilation of several entire nations, will depend on how each of us reacts to this act of His Mercy. At a time when the world has lost its sense of sin, we will suddenly see ourselves as God sees us. We will recognize our sins. If we reject this act of Mercy, if we then persist in our sins, will we not deserve the world purged with fire....or by whatever purging Divine Justice may elect." (1986, The Warning, 101 Foundation)

And perhaps better than anyone else, Father Bebie tells us why the illumination will come:

> The Warning prepares the Church. It is the most compelling preparation the Lord could have given us for the coming Age of Evangelization. By the "Warning," God demands that we face our sinfulness,

always the major obstacle to the spread of the Gospel, and repent. We must be purified. The Warning also reveals to us that our times are unique, unlike any other times, and that a new age is dawning for which we must be ready. There have been "wars and rumors of wars," and we have been tempted to panic, as if the end were at hand. But Jesus tells us, "that it is not yet the end" (Matthew 24:6). "This good news of the kingdom will be proclaimed to all the nations. Only after that will the end come" (Matthew 24:16). Could it be that he was referring to the Age of Evangelization we have been describing? ...The least we may infer from these declarations is that if they are accurate in their assessment of our moment of history, a great and final epoch is about to begin: The Era of Peace and the Age of Evangelization. The Warning is the "sign of the times" which announces to us the "New Times" the period of history when God will act in greater power than ever before to bring the Gospel, through His Church, to every creature. All will come to love the Hearts of Jesus and Mary, and love will reign in the world. The Warning is the first of these acts of power. It is preparing us all for the age of glory that is approaching.

Although Father Bebie died in 1986, his vision was timeless, for he saw that the illumination of consciences would spark "the great evangelization of the world." (See Epilogue: *After the Warning* by Fr. Bebie.) This is the same evangelization many prophets over the centuries have foretold would embrace the world at some point before the end of time. It is what the Era of Peace Mary predicted at Fatima would be all about, wrote Father Bebie. Now, only time and mankind's response to God's call separate Fr. Bebie's words from reality.

But there also remains the question of how this event will create such an impact. We will attempt to answer that question to some degree by examining more of the prophecies surrounding this foretold miracle of conscience and the words of some who claim to have already experienced a "judgment" that illuminated their soul in a way such as the coming miracle is promised to do.

***

BISHOP CLOSES INVESTIGATION OF GARABANDAL

Some people have been coming directly to the Diocese of Santander (Spain) asking about the alleged apparitions of Garabandal and especially for the answer about the position of the hierarchy of the Church concerning these apparitions. I need to communicate that:

1. All the bishops of the dioceses since 1961 through 1970 agreed that there was no supernatural validity for the apparitions.

2. In the month of December of 1977, Bishop Del Val of Santander, in union with his predecessors, stated that in the six years of being Bishop of Santander there were no new phenomena.

3. The same bishop, Del Val, let a few years go by to allow the confusion or fanaticism to settle down, and then after a few more years he initiated a commission to examine the apparitions in more depth. The conclusion of the commission agreed with the findings of the previous bishops, that there was no supernatural validity to such apparitions.

4. At the time of the conclusion of the study I was installed bishop in the diocese, in 1991. So during my visit to Rome, the *ad limina* visit which happened in the same year, I presented to the congregation for the Doctrine of the Faith the study and I asked for pastoral direction concerning this case.

5. On November 28, 1992, the Congregation sent me an answer saying that after examining the documentation, there was no need for direct intervention (by the Vatican) to take away the

jurisdiction of the ordinary Bishop of Santander in this case. Such a right belongs to the ordinary. Previous declarations of the Holy See agree in this finding. In the same letter they suggested that if I find it necessary to publish a declaration, that I reconfirm that there were no supernatural phenomena in the alleged apparitions, and this will make a unanimous position with my predecessors.

6.   Given that the declarations of my predecessors who studied the case have been clear and unanimous, I don't find it necessary to have a new public declaration that would raise notoriety about something which happened so long ago. However, I find it necessary to rewrite this report as a direct answer to the people who ask for direction concerning this question, which is now finished: I accept the decision of my predecessors and I appropriate (agree with) the direction of the Holy See.

7.   In reference to the Eucharistic celebration in Garabandal, following the decision of my predecessors, I ruled that Masses can be celebrated only in the parish church and there will be no references to the alleged apparitions and visiting priests who want to say Mass must have approval from the pastor, who has my authorization.

It's my wish that this information is helpful to you.

My regards in Christ,

José Vilaplana
Bishop of Santander
October 1996

*"During this time,
each one will see what he has
done during his whole life."*

- The Virgin Mary
to Amparo Cuevos of Escorial, Spain

Amparo Cuevos

CHAPTER SEVEN

CONTEMPORARY REVELATIONS

"From the heavens, you pronounced sentence, the earth was terrified and reduced to silence. When you arose, O God, for judgment to deliver the afflicted of the land."

— Ps 76:9-10

Anumber of reported visionaries claim messages concerning the coming miracle of conscience. The following are just a few that have occurred over the last several decades.

On April 5, 1968, Jesus reportedly told Rosa Quattrini, known as Mama Rosa, a celebrated visionary from San Damiano, Italy; **"I will come in triumph, I will come to 'give light to brighten all souls.' But it will be too late for those who do not understand the love of a mother. They will be in the midst of a terrible trial."** Then on August 5, 1968, Jesus reportedly told Rosa; **"I will soon come with 'a great light to convert a lot of souls,' and then Heaven and earth will tremble at my power. Then all souls will see 'the light' and all hearts will be set aflame with love for Me."**

Ten years later, the stigmatist Elena Lombardi of Rome, Italy, reported that on April 2, 1976, the Virgin Mary told her **"many signs never before seen will occur in the world as a warning to men to tell them that the measurer is filled. There will come —a fearful moment when my Son will speak with His judge's voice and pronounce the verdict over an anxious and drugged**

humanity." Six months after, on September 20, 1976, Jesus again told Mother Elena about the coming illumination: **"My left hand points to the 'warning' and my right hand, to the 'miracle.'**

On January 14, 1983, the Virgin Mary reportedly told the Spanish stigmatist Amparo Cuevos of Escorial, Spain, that **"during this time—each one will see—what he has done during his whole life."** Three years later, in Philadelphia, on September 8, 1986, the Blessed Virgin Mary reportedly told a visionary named Marianne (pseudonym), that **"many will fall down on their knees in anguish as they will see Whom they have pierced! It is the ultimate victory, the Cross that illuminates the path of all good will."**

In a message confirming how this miracle of the conscience may actually be a painful experience for some, Jesus reportedly told the anonymous American visionary of the *"Jesus King of All Nations"* devotion, **"Sin and evils committed by mankind are too great. No longer will I spare My Judgment to correct the conscience of mankind as a whole"** (February 20, 1989).

At Cold Spring, Kentucky, on December 20, 1992, the Virgin Mary reportedly delivered a message that clearly defined "the illumination": **"Soon a time will come when each one shall undergo a personal and individual view into their own soul, and they will see their weaknesses and their falsehoods. Every soul shall undergo this— with no exceptions. Then they will have a choice."**

That same year, on July 28, 1992, in Denver, Colorado, Jesus reportedly told a visionary named Veronica Garcia about the coming "illumination": **"Soon will be the time when all of My children will see Me. They will then be asked to make their choice. They will be shown the depths of their souls and will be frightened at what they shall see. The proud will be uprooted; the rich will be left with nothing. Only My meek and humble lambs**

will survive the great test. I come to you now so that you may warn them."

***

THREE SPECIAL VOICES SPEAK OF THE ILLUMINATION

Since the early 1990's, there have been more prophecies of the miracle of the illumination of all consciences. The messages of three individuals especially stand out concerning this coming miracle: Barbara Centilli, a mother, teacher, and housewife from Michigan; Fr. Stefano Gobbi, a priest from Italy; and Matthew Kelly, a young man from Australia. These three individuals have all received revelations that appear to explain in greater detail the prophesied miracle of conscience. Their revelations also appear to reveal that the fulfillment of this event is very near, perhaps closer than anyone can imagine. Let us look at each of these individuals and their messages.

"A change of heart is needed and only with powerful intervention will the "Awakening" come. Tenderness and gentle whispers have not accomplished My plan—the return of My children. "

- God the Father to Barbara Centilli

Eternal Father
by Gerry Simboli

CHAPTER EIGHT

BARBARA CENTILLI

"That is why I told you that you will die in your sins. For if you do not believe that I AM, you will die in your sins." So they said to him, "Who are you? "Jesus said to them, "What I told you from the beginning. I have much to say about you in condemnation. But the one who sent me is true, and what I heard from him I tell the world." They did not realize that he was speaking to them of the Father."
— Jn 8: 25- 27

S ince 1996, an American woman named Barbara Centilli has reported messages from God the Father that are quite profound. Over the last four years, many of the revelations appear to speak of the coming illumination of conscience. These messages have been published in three books titled, *Seeing With the Eyes of the Soul, Volumes* I-III. (St. Andrews Publications, McKees Rocks, Pa.)

Barbara Rose Centilli was 44 years of age when she began to record what she believed to be the voice of the Eternal Father speaking to her in prayer. Prior to this, her life was quite ordinary. Except for a few special experiences she believed to be of God, her life as a mother, grandmother, teacher, and wife were typical of the average American woman of her generation.

Barbara grew up in a small town in Michigan and eventually settled after marriage in a midwestern state. After graduating from college, she attended graduate school and worked as a teacher from the late 1970's through the early 1990's. During this period she raised four children and became involved with research and educational projects for students with special needs. Beginning in the mid-1990's, Barbara began to record in the form of a dialogue her prayerful conversations with God the Father, to whom she had developed a special devotion over her lifetime. These journals were eventually destroyed on the recommendation of a spiritual advisor who told her God does not speak to people in this manner.

However, in 1996, Barbara again began to record her conversations with the Father. By this time, she noticed God's responses to her in prayer were becoming very clear and distinct within her. She could hear His voice "in her heart and mind" and began to experience visions that sometimes accompanied the Father's words. Furthermore, as she reconciled and confronted what was happening to her, she became certain her experiences were not self-induced or imaginative but rather something she had no control over within herself.

It would not be possible to fully address the extraordinary contents of the revelations given to her. They cover a range of topics and are rich in detail concerning Barbara's interior life with God. However, the essence of them is unmistakable. The Father is requesting that through His Church all mankind be returned to Him. His home, He says, is all creation and His children must begin to come home to Him at this time. They must abandon any fear of Him and must know that He is all love and all mercy. It is His love that has especially been given as the reason for the coming illumination.

The Eternal Father also tells Barbara that the end of an era is about to dawn upon the world and that these are truly prophetic times. Most significantly, the long awaited Triumph of the Church is about to be fulfilled. This is the "Triumph" Mary promised at Fatima in 1917, and according to the Father's words to Barbara, will now come. The Father also revealed to Barbara His desire for His children to consecrate themselves to Him and that the Catholic Church declare a Feast Day in His name.

Barbara Centilli is under spiritual direction and the Catholic Chuch in her diocese has opened an investigation.

The following revelations appear to involve the coming miracle of the illumination of consciences, and especially why God—in His great love for His children—has ordained such a moment in history. The revelations, taken as a whole, seem to present a "theological" understanding of the miracle in addition to conveying a prophetic assurance of its reality:

***

The time is ripe. My will will come down among My people and there will be mercy with justice. ...Intercede—look about you. Who do you love? My love will save them. Be My instruments in all times and in all places. (August 27, 1996)

***

Remember, child, all is well within My heart...stop, listen. The crashing of the waves. The pounding of sea, sound breaking over rocks...The time has come for the reckoning of mankind—a reunion with its Father. You have all been away a very long time. The call is on, the crashing and the calling—but to hear the call, broken over the rocks, the hard, hard rocks, you must be in the silence and dark of the night. You've always known this. (September 11, 1996)

***

Do you think I have abandoned you? No, never, My tiny rose. Ready to bloom. I am here by your side ready to bring down My Merciful wrath. For this "day" in time is over. Darkness is defeated. Look to the skies for your final salvation. The sign I promised is coming. Is come. Soon. Remember My words, daughter. Soon.

Seed. Seeds were planted at the beginning. Her seed and His seed. You were right to think that there was more than a behavioral/environmental basis for the sharp difference between good and evil in My children. That is why I sent My Son as the antidote to combat the dread disease of evil which has been passed down generation to generation. You have seen its effects played out in your own family. Every family. The drama of Eden has been played out in each generation, each family, each person. But I have loved you all.

I tell you this drama, this war, will not be played out until all My children have returned to Me as a family. I am gathering My children in My arms—like you, Barbara. Love them! I have put a savior in the midst of each family, each group—to love and to give mercy. Warrior: you are all warriors of My mercy. Absorb and transform. It hurts. It is painful. This transformation, spiritual re-creation of matter and soul. But it must be—to usher in My new era. The one promised. The one prophesied—has come. Only in retrospect will My children realize how "outside My will" these times have been. But the offenses have grieved Me—sorely, My daughter.   Enough!"
(October 23, 1996)

***

Listen very carefully. This is a time of many changes. Time is bending back upon itself. The Spirit wants to rush forward towards its ultimate end, only to be frustrated and turned back at every turn. ...To overcome the tremendous effects of generations of sin, I must send the power to break through and transform the world. But this surge of power will be uncomfortable, even painful for some. This will cause the contrast between darkness and light to become even greater. The attachment to what is darkness will be even more painful. As in the scene in Exodus where My children had to choose. This is happening now.

The Spiritual contamination will affect the mind and body as well. Many will become ill with a disorder that can only be cured by conversion. For some, the conversion will come too late. This plague will be unleashed soon so that the weeding process can begin. It is not by bombs or war that man's demise will come, but rather through his own spiritual corruption. Mary's children will have immunity to this disease. I tell you this so that you may prepare: prayer, fasting, and penance. What have you learned, My child? You are called to live what I live. I have spared you from none of the pain so that you can share in joy someday. (November 15, 1996)

***

Soon all will be transformed. Sooner than you think. What joy that within your lifetime the change will take place. Be ready. Be vigilant. I come swiftly to bring Mine back home to Me.   This is the transformation—when I come to make My home and all is transformed. .... All things are possible in the Lord. You must take time with the One you love. Give yourself completely and do not hold back. I am present in all those who call Me Father. Recognize that. (December 16, 1996)

***

The time is upon us when all questions will be answered. From your side drops the blood of My Son Jesus, for you are with Us. Immolate the sacrifice. Be one with Us. Sleep now and remember My Words: all that is present will cease and become new. All will be transformed in Me, your One true God—now and forever. Be not ashamed if you wander in confusion. The time has come for impact. All is thrown in disarray. But all that is Mine will be drawn to Me. Through you, some will be saved. Ask for them by name. This is your responsibility before your Lord. ..." (February 1, 1997)

***

Soon all this will be over. You are right in assuming that by yourself you can do nothing. I AM with you. But the transformation must take place. Without this, My children will continue to lose their way and be lost. (February 11, 1997)

***

Awakening. This is a time of awakening and renewal. Make use of all I put in your path. Time is limited. Look to Me for your solace and comfort.

There is a door that is yet unopened. It remains closed because of your lack of Faith. You must believe in miracles. And I will bless you with them. Life is short. Please do what I ask of you, daughter. What is My will? What do I will for My children? I will that they inherit My Kingdom. (February 14, 1997)

***

Yes, and what of your brothers and sisters? They must come, too. How can this be done, My little one?....Memories come back to you. This is a re-awakening. A softening of hearts. This is the miracle I foretold through My prophet—Isaiah: 'A time will come when hearts will be opened up to the Lord…prior to My coming.'

I am coming among you even now in a new way. ...I am coming to dwell in the hearts of My children. But they must be ready. They must be prepared. This union, this joining, is possible only through consecration to me. Body, mind, and soul—the will!" (April 29, 1997)

***

Rest assured, my little rose, there will be no other time in history like this. This is my final invitation and triumph—through your Mother, through My Son Jesus, and through My Holy Spirit. These are the times spoken of in Ezechial 3:17. Now go, My child, and see what your Father tells you. (June 5, 1997)

***

I call Mine home in these times. I have waited and now is the time. To hesitate would result in the loss of more of My little ones. The transformation must begin, and has, but to accomplish this, I ask that "My children" work with their Father for this end—the transformation—a new Heaven and new earth: the new Jerusalem. Only I know the time and the date. My children need only know this: the transformation begins, drawing down Almighty God from Heaven, transforming the earth and all that is in it. My purifying and transformative love and power will change the face of all that is. And so it should be. This is My will—that all remain with and in Me, in the rhythm and harmony of My will. Oh, what a splendor that the human mind cannot even begin to comprehend, Barbara, My little rose.

For most, they will feel the power of Almighty God course through their being: body, mind, and soul. They should recognize this as the transformative process. As My children they are to offer all things to Me in love so that I may transform them. See one reality superimposed over the other, matter and being remade, made anew. For My plan to be accomplished, My power must be grounded in and directed through My children. Do you understand this?

The speed and efficiency of this process depends on the response of My children. My children will feel the suffering of themselves and others as they offer it to Me.   But those outside My will will experience another kind of suffering. A suffering caused by the transformation and incorporation of all into My will. For many of My children, this has been a slow process—far gentler than what awaits those that refused My will. Pray for these, little daughter. Pray ardently and unceasingly for them. (June 9 1997)

***

A change of heart is needed and only with powerful intervention will the awakening come. Tenderness and gentle whispers have not accomplished My plan—the return of My children.   Speak to My children before I must thunder a reply to their deaf ears and darkened ways. (November 11, 1997)

***

You are where I want you, My daughter. Spreading the light of this—the final devotion. The light which pierces the darkness in these times. There will be no other. For this is why you were created. Each child was brought into the world so each one could return to its source, it's Father. That is why I come now through you to hold My standard high, high above the crowds, the chaos, the din. Let My children see it. Let them rally round it. And bring to Me a palm branch as tribute and a pledge—that you are Mine. Man stands inside or outside My will. There is no middle ground, no in-between. He is in Me or he is outside Me. And the storm approaches. I am calling My children home in this time. Touch your hand to My heart. Feel the rhythm of My divine will. Let this be the music that draws My children. The rhythm and harmony of My divine will. (November 27, 1997)

***

Cry out as one crying out in the desert. Time is short and I will come like a transforming fire of My light and love. My merciful justice will be visited upon the earth. All must be ready in their hearts. They must welcome Me into the temple of their hearts. ...I must be present with and in My children. Heaven will touch earth. Those who carry the presence of God will be saved and renewed—they will be transformed. (December 27, 1997)

***

The Archangel Raphael: Love the Lord, adore Him, praise Him on this day which is a gift to His children. Banish all thoughts of frustration and disappointment. Consider this day an oasis in the desert. Sing praise to your Creator, your Father, your God. And rest safely in His heart as He rests in yours. This pleases Him mightily. The day of the Lord approaches. All must be prepared. Ready yourselves in body, mind, and soul. Purify yourselves. Avail yourselves of the Holy Sacraments and preach the Good News; God is with us, come down from Heaven. This is your Father's most fervent desire to be with His children. But most have forgotten Him.

This you know. They must be re-introduced. This is the time. (February 6, 1998)

***

... Remain closely aligned with My divine will. Listen and you will hear My drum beat. The countdown begins. My glory will be made manifest in ways that will elicit wonder and awe. For this is the time of all times. This is the time of the Eternal Father—the Father of all mankind. And I bring Peace to My children, Israel—for it is time. ... You are like David with the rock. You, too, will do great things for the glory of your God. Test this premise. Read: 2 Sm 7:14-23—Read and know who you are:" (February 16, 1998)

***

Think. Think for a moment. In passing from one stage to the other there is discomfort. But this will pass, as do all unpleasantries. Time is transitory—I am eternal. My presence in the world becomes clearer to My children, all. The radiance of My being is reflected in My creation and lives in the souls of My children. As I have told you, the transformation has begun— only to be more fully realized. The steps to your Father are shorter now by contrast to times past. The time before restoration shortens. The sanctuary light dims—seemingly—but only for a moment. All must be prepared and readied for the coming of the Father—for the return of My children, all.

Despite the frustration and the stumbling blocks, the

time approaches when My children may know, love, and honor their Father—through their own choice. All is being readied for this triumph. The passage from one era, one time into the next, unfolds—mightily. Go not against the heart and will of the Father Who calls you all by name. Is it not My promise that all who approach Me in love will indeed find themselves home—restored to the One Who loves them? (March 14, 1998)

***

Time is so very short, little one. My light comes to the world but for a time before renewal in a blast of transformation. Ready yourselves. Purify and cleanse yourselves. Strip yourselves of all that is not of Me. The time begins for choices in this critical period. Move toward My light. Align yourselves with My holy will. Be in harmony with the music of your God. (March 30, 1998)

***

The force of My hand will come swiftly and justly—but always, it comes with mercy. Did I not allow my prodigal son to feel the consequences of his choices and actions? And so it will be in these times. There are consequences in the Divine Order that serve as My justice—but also My mercy. For in experiencing consequences, My children often see their way clear to come home to their Father. This is not a bad thing, little one. This is my goodness and mercy shining forth to My children. You have been made to feel the consequences of this culture—in your choices and the choices of those around you. Your life is an intersection of all such choices and consequences. (April 7 1998)

***

Little one, what I tell you is true. Did I not tell you I would come? Have you such little Faith. Great and wondrous times are upon you. They are closer than you think. There is no reason to fear. What has been overlooked in what you research? It was all much simpler than was thought. Man makes the approach to the Creator more difficult than was intended.

[I see a book of Holy Scripture. It is opened to what seems to be the middle. In the middle is the Parable of the Prodigal Son. As if the book is transparent, I see at the beginning, the first three chapters of the Book of Genesis. At the end, I see the Book of Revelations—the Apocalypse. The Parable of the Prodigal Son is the central focus in what I see with connections to the Book of Genesis and the Book of Revelations.]

See the story projected [from The Parable of the Prodigal Son] forward [toward the front of the book] to Genesis and backward [toward the back of the book] to Revelations—all from the Parable of the Prodigal Son. See it this way once more as was given you. *[I see it again.]*

See? So much more will be explained to you now. Search for the answers to questions that must be answered in this time. I bring you all out of bondage. The time has come for the children of God to be reconciled with their Father. Remember, I come as a thief in the night. Be ready. And tell all those you come in contact with that their Father approaches. As My Son Jesus is likened to the Morning Star, so too with the Father—I am the Morning Sun. Remember, I have told you that after the sun sets, it also rises. And so with this time. Shalom. Sleep in the peace of your Lord God and Father. (April 27, 1998)

***

The Triumph is imminent. Know this and prepare. Prepare for this time. Ready yourselves, for My hand will pass over all Creation in a gesture of merciful justice. This will take place sooner than you think. For I can be separated from My children no longer. Respond to the signs given to you. They are powerful and plenty. You have only to open your eyes and see, your ears and hear, your heart and love. Be alive in this culture of death. Be alive, my children. To love is to live. To love is to obtain life—in your Father. Now go in My peace, little one, My rose. And remember My promise. I will be with you always— you are Mine. (May 8, 1998)

***

Expressed in simple terms, I speak of My children returning home to Me. Where I am, so is Heaven, so is Paradise, so is the New Jerusalem. As I have explained to you before, little one, the Kingdom will not come from without but from within. How can it ever come if My children refuse to see it, acknowledge it? Even more, they must want it. How many of My children acknowledge that it exists?

How many bid it come? How can they? They have no knowledge or belief in it. When the cutting edge of truth slices through the illusion that is the world, those who are not prepared will have difficulty in adjusting to the light which will penetrate powerfully into each and every soul. (May 12, 1998)

***

Seek your Father now in these times as the curtain of Heaven will soon be drawn back and a flood of glory will encompass the earth. In this, you may be assured. All glory and honor are due your Heavenly Father. Ready yourselves, My children, and know that I AM Your God and Father. No more will My children wander disconsonantly without direction or purpose. The family of God is to be reunited. An awareness of God will settle over the earth as in no other time. Ready yourselves, My children. Be right with your Lord. Choose life in your Creator. Choose your Father. The time approaches when you must bend your knees and present your hearts to the One Who made you in His image—for one purpose only: to know, love, and honor God Your Father. (May 25, 1998)

***

Daughter, the time of conversion approaches when all will see great light—many will be called in this time. God chooses Whom He will. Theirs is the choice to respond. And you will call upon those who will see the Light of God, their hearts pierced by the Love of God. My peace, littlest daughter. (June 12, 1998)

***

This is how it will be, Barbara Rose. See and believe. The time is short and all mankind must choose. Teach them to call out to Me—and I will come to them. I will be present to them. This is not complicated. My love for My children is a simple truth—perhaps too simple for some to grasp. They crave complication. My children are as in a deep sleep and must now awaken to the truth. My reality may be comforting or stinging—depending on the response of My children. This is My will. I repeat: Draw down the mercy of your God. Call Me to yourselves in this time. Believe, have faith and trust in your Father. Know that I am with you always. Turn not away from My face any longer. Stand not in the shadows, in the darkness. Turn around toward the light. Call Me by name—"God, My Father." This is what I have waited for, for all time. Now be at peace. I will triumph. Of this, have no doubt. Come to Me— now!" (August 19, 1998)

***

There are so many opportunities in your life that bring you close to Me—suffering is only one. You are also close to Me in the service and care of others. Remain with Me, little one. Soon—the dawn of a new day to be remembered. These times will be but a distant memory.   Already the transformation begins—in earnest. This is the time awaited for in holy Scripture. When the holy prophet Ezechial said the trumpet will sound—apply this to your times and be attentive. My sword— [I see the image of Our Father picking up the little child and in so doing, He must put His sword down in the earth. The sun sets over the mountain tops—it is setting. Our Father stoops down and comforts the child. The child is crying and lost.] You are dear to Me, daughter. Remember My words well — the day of your Lord God is upon you all. Tremble in fear or tremble from love. All will be Mine. Stay close to Me in prayer throughout the day, little one—in My peace. (September 27, 1998)

***

I am calling you, My children, to be close to Me— now in this day, in this hour, in this minute. For the time is close when I will call you in a new and different way. No more will you claim that your eyes could not see and your ears would not hear. For I will come upon you as a great and terrible light in the darkness. Are your eyes adjusted to the light? Have your ears adjusted to My voice? Earthly sensations are but a passing thing. But what I bring is secondary only to My holy and undisputed will—I bring Myself to you as a tender Father, tending to His little ones, gathering them in this day, in this hour, in this minute. Each heartbeat signals My presence—the rhythm and harmony of My divine will. Acknowledge that your Father is at hand. Offer yourselves to Me—know Me, love Me, honor Me. Consecrate yourselves to Me, your Father, and I will surely come to you. Unbidden, I come powerfully but unexpected. How difficult this will be for those who do not know Me. The day of your Lord is at hand. Bend your knee to the one who created you. And I will give you peace in My kingdom. (December 15, 1998)

***

The tomb is open, daughter—and the sun is risen. A new day begins for the world. Peace and the love of God is given freely to those who embrace it in these times. Is this unusual? Surely it is when compared to times past. There is a reason, little one of My heart. Push away those that drink in the world. Let them imbibe their worldly pleasures, becoming drunk on passions that will fade and pass with time. You be the light and let those who will dare to come, come—and be amazed at what the Lord their God will do for them. This is clear in Scripture, is it not? Examine what has been said in Ephesians 5:17-30. What do I say? I say bring My children to Myself and let them drink in My glory—let it shine through them to the world so that all may be transformed and made new in Me. How can this be done? Through Love. How simple you might say. But how powerful! There is more power in willed love than in all the force that can be violently exerted. It is the undoing of all that is darkness and evil in this cold, bereft world. Love brings warmth and light to renew. Yes, this is difficult, child. But so necessary to My plan. Righteousness shall apply to all in the day which is Mine.

An abrupt transition will take place for all to see and experience—and then the reaction to choose. But what will the reaction of My children be in this time? Only love, My dearest daughter. Only love. And so I tell you to weep no more. Dry your eyes as I dry them with My compassionate mercy. Let the truth unfold and blanket the earth—covering all. And those that it touches will be glad and rejoice for they have been touched by your Lord

God and Father—Myself revealed. Now be ready for what I send you. Respond with an open heart. Soon, daughter, soon. (April 4, 1999)

***

Why do I tell you this? So that you will understand what will soon transpire. And what is this? Because of your lack of love, My children, for your God, for each other, and for yourselves, I need to draw you closer to Myself—with a kiss that will awaken you from a long and empty sleep. You slumber yet, immune to the truth that has been given to you in this time. But you will soon see the power of your God unfold before your eyes. Then and only then will you truly see that I am truly God. Now remember My genuine and most sincere love for you. You, each and every child, are the desire of My heart, made new in your Father. Much will yet take place in this year of your Father and God, Creator of All." (May 5, 1999)

***

But a day approaches when I will intervene for the good of you all—I will draw back My mercy so that you might feel the consequences of your own choices. Soon, daughter, very soon. Do you hear Me? I come soon. Deliberate on nothing more than this: what do I choose before the Lord, my God? How can I know, love, and honor my heavenly Father? I have answered these questions with My peace. (May 10, 1999)

***

In this time of trials in the world, mankind looks for comfort and assurance that all will be well. But where is mankind looking? Not to Me, the Father, little one. And that is, after all, the answer—as you so well know. How do we remedy this grave situation, this loss of faith in this time? It can only come by the power of My Holy Spirit permeating the world and man. But these, My children, must choose this course, this option, to attain the fullness of graces offered to them in this time. We will see the coming of a great challenge and all in their own way will choose, as they must in every moment.

Am I not with you, My children, in every place, every moment? A time of realization is at hand and then all will know that I AM. I come to each child as a loving Father—the most loving and merciful Father—to wipe away their tears and crush their fears in My mighty hands, loved away in My gentle embrace. I AM the Father of you all and I passionately desire that intimacy between Father and child be born in this time—a tenderness that endures all difficulties. Now listen, My children, when I tell you that you will know that I AM truly with you when you cast your eyes to the heavens and see the sun of My love rising on your darkened world. This love of Mine for My children will be manifested by a sign that will broach no misinterpretation. All will be clear. The sun of My love will rise in your souls not to be eclipsed by the evil of the world.

Never hesitate to approach Me, your gentle Father, in the midst of your distress. For My paternal arms are open to you always. Now believe this: I AM your one,

true God and Father—and I come for My children in this time. For they are Mine and there will be peace once more. (May 11 1999)

***

This is the way of My love—acknowledgment and recognition through My Spirit surely placed within you, the passive action of your soul to receive your God, your inheritance as children of the Most High. When you see Me, when you hear Me, when you touch Me, it is because I live in you and have claimed you for My own. Does a man relinquish what he has claimed? Can "I" lose what is Mine? This surely would be imperfect weakness on My part. But it is not so. Am I not perfect? There is no carelessness in My regard for you, in My care as a Father.

[I see our Father holding two children and He looks into their eyes and I can feel the intensity of love He feels for these children and I know they will never be parted—because our Father lives in them and God cannot be separated from God. I see our Father lead the children through thick brush to the rise over a great water and the sun is huge and seems to be sitting on the water.]

"Father, what does this mean?

[One child is constantly looking up at our Father. The other one is very quiet and seems distant, distracted. Our Father lowers the child into the great water (of His mercy) and the child sinks in it and doesn't try to swim.]

This is the great miracle of the sun, My sun, My power, My light—I will kiss the great oceans of mercy with My energy which is light, which is My power, which is My glory—to enliven those who have succumbed to death. I will gift them with My warm and loving presence—this is My mercy. After the cleansing action of My mercy will come the life of My Spirit, powerful and transmitted, conducted, through the waters of My mercy. Those who are overwhelmed by My mercy will yet live. Do you not yet see the parallel, My child? One son stays and one son goes. But I have provided for both in My own way—enlivening through My Spirit those who have died in the flesh— those who do not know they are dead inside—even they will know My restorative power. A reawakening is at hand—timely in measure and true to My words: Thy Kingdom come, thy will be done on earth as it is in Heaven. These words I gave you through My Son. And much needed in a world dead to My presence. Arise, little ones—and believe! Blessed be he who honors his Father and His Son in My Holy Spirit. Shalom. (December 28, 1999)

***

Now meditate on what this means in the upcoming year. Your fiat is given when you love Me as Father. Did not your Mother Mary and your Savior Jesus give "Me" their Fiat? To Me it must be given: "Thy Will be done on earth as it is in Heaven." Let there be no mistake, Barbara Rose—this simple and heartfelt fiat is the key to the new millennium, to the new era, to the next century.

Barbara, your places are set. You need only respond to the invitation. And when you come to the table, feast thankfully and joyfully, spreading good will and cheer. The door will be left open so others may be drawn to the light. Beckon them in. Be hospitable. There is room for all at My table. There is room for the entire family of God. Some will cower, some will hesitate. But all will see the light of this great feast. Call them in joyously, praising Your one true God and Father. Peace on earth for this time of times. Shalom. (December 31, 1999)

***

The Romans conquered the world. I will conquer the souls of man. This is My Kingdom. And the external will be manifest, reflecting the internal. Do you understand, child? First things first.

Concern yourself with My coming, for I come soon to be among My children in a new way, unforseen by man but foretold by your Mother.

I cannot let go of even one child—it grieves Me. I am tenacious in this regard, Barbara Rose. I protect My own, My children, with My grace and My powerful presence.

See Me in My little ones, in the poor, in the naked and afflicted. I am present with them always. For they recognize the need for Me and I come to them.

What will it take for the others, child? Think. What must I do so that all may believe? Is this not My purpose? To bring all My children to Myself? This is

not a game. This is My will. (February 22, 2000)

***

Daughter of My Heart:

Listen to My words to you in this moment. All things shall pass away. What does this mean?

I believe You are referring to the coming of the New Jerusalem and the transformation? All things made new?

Yes, but what in this instant does it mean—for you, my children?

That what is now will be changed and perfected?

This is so; what does it mean in your lives now?
That what we are we will not be?

Yes. So there are two important lessons here, Barbara Rose. First, what you are now —most beloved children on earth—you shall not be. You are as one who "will be transformed." Have you seen a butterfly emerge from a cocoon? This is likened to what shall take place—beauty, glorious beauty, unsurpassed, these souls of yours, who now dwell on earth. Joined as they will be to new form and being. This is what awaits you all if you have but the courage to see and believe.

Secondly, little one, this means, too, that what you will become is something you cannot imagine. What is this new state: it is wholeness and completion in and

with God—your Creator, Savior, and Sanctifier. Restored by the good will and graces of a Father who dotes on His children. I have not left you alone in your ignorance. I have come to you in My Son. I have sent you My Holy Spirit at His request. And I have given you the gentlest of mothers to help lead you to My Son—a Mother who grieves for those who do not understand what they really are—sons and daughters of God Almighty.

But, Father, does this have anything to do with the work I mentioned?

Believe Me when I tell you that I desire that this knowledge be clearly understood. If My children, all, really knew this truth, there would be no more wars, no more suffering among My children. They would clearly see who they are. How can they love each other when they do not know the object of their love?

Father, I don't know if I clearly know what You mean?

Penetrate into this mystery: When you die, you live truly in your God—if you believe with a pure heart.

Love, honor, and adore the One Who created you, Who cares for you, Who extends His gift of sharing in My Glory—but how?

By knowing, loving, and honoring You, Jesus, and the Holy Spirit?

Yes, but you must also love yourselves and all others. This is My Way. It is the only way to peace. Recognize My presence. Be alert.

I wait among the cocoons of death, lingering for the transformation of My children, restored to Me at long last.

Remember, child, the external reflects the internal: the physical, the spiritual. When will My Kingdom on earth truly reflect My Kingdom in Heaven? When will they be One? What must take place, Barbara Rose? A fiat of the heart—perfect, intact, beating in the rhythm and harmony of My divine will, waiting to bloom into new life. Shalom. My peace I give you.
(February 24, 2000)

***

One of Barbara Centilli's revelations concerning the future deserves a closer look. For years, some writers have forwarded the hypothesis that the great "Miracle of the Sun" at Fatima on October 13, 1917, in which the sun left its orbit and plunged towards the earth, was actually a foreshadowing sign of the coming miracle of an illumination of all consciences. In a message to Barbara Centilli on March 23, 1998, the Eternal Father appears to confirm this hypothesis. He explains that in both situations (the Oct 13, 1917, Miracle of the Sun at Fatima and the coming worldwide miracle of conscience), it actually was and will be again God's own "approach," concealed in the unfolding dynamics of the manifestation of both miracles, that the people at Fatima felt and soon all of mankind will experience. Moreover, it is God's closeness, His nearness that causes the response in a soul. The initial response being fear, then understanding and, finally, acceptance and love. Here is the March 23, 1998 message:

I place you beside Me tonight as I speak to you about many things. I am pleased that you have come to Me

in love and trust to share with Me what is in your heart. ... First of all, My daughter, you must realize by now the tightly woven bond which exists between this devotion to Me and the immediate steps leading up to the Triumph of your Mother's Immaculate Heart. Laid out in the scheme of mankind's salvation history is the end, the ultimate completion of this journey. Through your Mother's fiat, her "Yes," My Son Jesus came into the world to redeem My children, all. Now, the time approaches when this final Triumph will be realized. Do you know how this will come about?

I know it has to do with our return to You, Father. I believe Mary, our Mother, made this possible through Jesus.

Yes, this is true, daughter. You speak well. But all stops short of the eventual goal of the return of My children home to their Father. Only when I am recognized, loved, and honored by My children—all—will this Triumph be completed. Do you understand?

Father, are You saying that the Feast Day (for God Our Father) and Consecration is the Triumph?

You have spoken truly, little one. The return of My children is your Mother's Triumph. All My children must return unhindered to their one true God and Father. Then My Kingdom will have come on earth as it is in Heaven.

This process will be gradual, but it must begin now. ... Each of My children has their role to play in My plan for mankind. ... Yours to present to the world—now in this time.

I come to My children as was shown in the Miracle of the Sun at Fatima. I come so close to warm you and fill you with My light. Why does this frighten My children? Because they are not ready, they are not prepared. They are not able to see beyond their own preconceptions—their constructions of truth. I am Truth. And the approach of your God without proper preparation as outlined by your Mother is folly indeed. Purification must take place. A cleansing of hearts, bodies, and minds.

[I see an image of the Miracle of the Sun—the way the sun's rays seem to color and permeate everything they touch.]

See how I effused all that I touched (at Fatima). See how I chased away the gloom and discomfort. I am light and love. And I bring with Me a power that will transform. All will be transformed in the Lord. I was present at the Miracle of Fatima—in graphic depiction of what could have been and what will be yet!

But, Father, in the Miracle of the Sun, what of St. Joseph? What of the Holy Spirit?

St. Joseph, My good and tender son, represented the Fatherly arms that hold and behold My Son Jesus—as I desire to hold all of you. The Spirit, My Spirit, was represented in the rays of the sun penetrating all of My creation. The miracle was not as great as it could have been. I withdrew from My children as they shrank away in terror from the power and glory of their God. Even then many forget the impact of this experience. Yes, daughter, I am represented in the sun as you see clearly in Holy Scripture, My Word. The power of the sun gives life, but it has also been harnessed by man, in aping God, to take life away. Life or chastisement. How will the power of God be used?

I wait patiently, oh, so patiently, to enter you and warm your souls in My love. But as with all My gifts, even this has been abused and will be again in chastisement if My little ones do not find their way back home to their Father. At Fatima you saw the options and reactions played out. Approach Me in love and trust and you have nothing to fear. I showed you this at Fatima. See and believe!

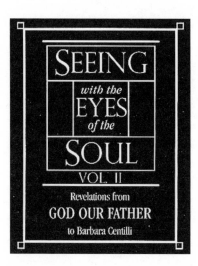

Seeing with the Eyes of the Soul, Vol. I,II,III
Published by St. Andrew's Productions.

"A new fire will come down from Heaven and will purify all humanity, which has become pagan. It will be like a Judgment in Miniature, and each one will see himself in the light of the very Truth of God."

- The Virgin Mary to Fr. Stefano Gobbi

Fr. Stefano Gobbi and Pope John Paul II.

CHAPTER NINE

FR. STEFANO GOBBI

"Thus, the word of the Lord came to me: Son of Man, I have appointed you a watchman for the House of Israel. When you hear a word from my mouth, you shall warn them for me."

— Ez 3:17

Fr. Stefano Gobbi was 42 years old and living in Milan, Italy, when he received his first "interior locution." He entered the priesthood late in life and was ordained in 1964 after working in real estate and insurance. Then, in 1973, his life changed radically. The priest received a sign and was led to understand that the Virgin Mary's messages to him were intended especially for priests. Consequently, the Marian Movement of Priests was born, and in 28 years, the organization has attracted tens of thousands of priests, bishops, and cardinals, as well as millions of laity worldwide.

For years, Fr. Gobbi traveled the world, holding cenacles and prayer retreats. He was tireless. Visiting almost every country in the world, he moved constantly forward toward the approaching fulfillment of the times. It is a fulfillment that appears to have unfolded step by step in Mary's messages to him. Fr. Gobbi's messages are considered extraordinary, far beyond what most visionaries receive. Most of all, the messages are directly linked to the Virgin Mary's words at Fatima. For it was at Fatima's "Chapel of the Apparitions" that Fr. Gobbi first experienced an "interior force" and the inspiration to begin his work. Soon, Mary was reportedly giving him messages that were profound, startling, and immensely prophetic. (The messages have received an imprimatur from one Cardinal and several bishops.)

The times at hand, Mary's messages to Fr. Gobbi explained, are described in the Book of Revelation. Other messages foretold with astonishing accuracy the unfolding of human events over the last three decades, events such as the fall of communism in Eastern Europe and the dismantling of the Soviet Union. From AIDS to a coming conversion of Japan to Christianity, the Virgin Mary's prophecies to Fr. Gobbi are overwhelming in their detail. Mary has even reportedly revealed in her messages the contents of the Third Part of the Secret of Fatima, something the world has anxiously awaited since 1960, but which have never been disclosed.

But more than anything else, Mary's messages to Father Stefano Gobbi have significantly defined how the invisible world is wreaking havoc on the visible world, how the tragic events of this century can only be correctly understood in spiritual terms, and how the foretold climax of this period, the apostasy predicted at Fatima in the revealed portion of the Third Secret, is now visible for all to see. Indeed, the very basis for the messages appears to be this apostasy, especially in the priesthood. Curiously, Father Gobbi had gone to Fatima on pilgrimage that first day and was praying for some priests who, besides having personally given up their vocations, were attempting to form themselves into associations in rebellion against Church authority.

In her messages, the Virgin Mary explained to Fr. Gobbi that over the last two centuries the world has truly witnessed what was foretold at La Salette, France, in 1846 to Melanie Calvat and Maximim Giraud. The many wars and the great genocide, the messages state, speaks for itself as confirmation. Likewise, the gradual escalation of the power of evil in the world, as foretold at La Salette, is undeniably visible for anyone with spiritual sense.

According to Marian writers and theologians, Father Gobbi's messages also crystalize the story of the century-long reign of Satan. In lieu of this understanding, Mary's messages to Fr. Gobbi have defined what must still occur, including the miracle of illumination of all consciences.

From 1988 through 1996, Father Stefano Gobbi of Italy received five messages from the Virgin Mary concerning the coming illumination of consciences:

<u>May 22, 1988, Feast of Pentecost:</u>

Beloved sons, gather together from every part of the earth to live this feast day in the cenacle of my Immaculate Heart. This day which recalls the descent of the Holy Spirit upon the Apostles, gathered together in prayer with me in the Cenacle of Jerusalem. On this day of Pentecost of the Marian Year, consecrated to me, I am calling upon you to unite your prayer to that of your heavenly Mother, to obtain the great gift of the Second Pentecost. The time of the Second Pentecost has come.

The Holy Spirit will come, as a heavenly dew of grace and of fire, which will renew all the world. Under his irresistible action of love, the Church will open itself to live the new era of its greatest holiness and will shine resplendently with so strong a light that it will attract to itself all the nations of the earth.

The Holy spirit will come, that the will of the heavenly Father be accomplished and the created universe once again reflect his great glory.

The Holy spirit will come, to establish the glorious reign of Christ and it will be a reign of grace, of holiness, of love, of justice and of peace. WITH HIS DIVINE LOVE, HE WILL OPEN THE DOORS OF HEARTS AND ILLUMINATE ALL CONSCIENCES. EVERY PERSON WILL SEE HIMSELF IN THE BURNING FIRE OF DIVINE TRUTH. IT WILL BE LIKE A JUDGMENT IN MINIATURE. AND THEN JESUS CHRIST WILL BRING HIS GLORIOUS REIGN IN THE WORLD.

The Holy Spirit will come, by means of the triumph of my Immaculate Heart. For this, I am calling upon you all today to enter into the cenacle of my heart. Thus, you will be prepared to receive the gift of the Holy Spirit which will transform you and make you the instruments with which Jesus will establish his reign.

***

October 2, 1992, Feast of the Holy Guardian Angels:

Today the angels of light of my Immaculate Heart are at your side, my beloved ones and children consecrated to me. This is their feast day. Honor them, call upon them, follow them, live always with them, they who have been given to you by the Heavenly Father, as your guardians and protectors.

Today is their time. This final period of the purification and the great tribulation corresponds with a particular and powerful manifestation of the angels of the Lord.

You have entered into the most painful and difficult phase of the battle between the Spirits of Good and the Spirits of Evil, between angels and the demons. It is a terrible struggle which is taking place around you and above you. You, poor earthly creatures, are caught up in it, and thus you experience the particularly powerful force of those snares which are set for you by the wicked spirits, in their attempt to lead you along the road of sin and evil.

And so these are the times when the action of your guardian angels must become still stronger and continuous. Pray to them often, listen to them with docility, follow them at every moment.

The cult of veneration and praise offered to the angels of the Lord must become more widespread and solemnly observed in the Church. For indeed, to them is reserved the task of making to you the much-awaited announcement of your proximate liberation.

The announcement of the three angels should be looked forward to by you with confidence, received with joy and followed with love.

Your liberation will coincide with the termination of iniquity, with the complete liberation of all creation from the slavery of sin and evil.

WHAT WILL COME TO PASS IS SOMETHING SO

VERY GREAT THAT IT WILL EXCEED ANYTHING THAT HAS TAKEN PLACE SINCE THE BEGINNING OF THE WORLD. IT WILL BE LIKE A JUDGMENT IN MINIATURE, AND EACH ONE WILL SEE HIS OWN LIFE AND ALL HE HAS DONE, IN THE VERY LIGHT OF GOD.

TO THE FIRST ANGEL THERE BEFALLS THE TASK OF MAKING THIS ANNOUNCEMENT TO ALL: "GIVE TO GOD GLORY AND OBEDIENCE; PRAISE HIM BECAUSE THE MOMENT HAS COME WHEN HE WILL JUDGE THE WORLD. GO DOWN ON YOUR KNEES BEFORE HIM WHO HAS MADE HEAVEN AND EARTH, THE SEA AND THE SPRINGS OF WATER.

Your liberation will coincide with the defeat of Satan and of every diabolical spirit.

All the demons and the spirits of the damned who, during these years have been poured out into every part of the world, for the ruin and damnation of souls, will be cast into hell, from which they have come, and they will no longer be able to do harm.

All the power of Satan will be destroyed.

To the second angel there befalls the task of making this announcement: 'Fallen is Babylon the great, she who made all the nations drink of the intoxicating wine of her prostitution.

Your liberation will coincide, above all, with the reward granted to all those who have remained faithful during the great trial, and with the great chastisement meted out to those who have allowed themselves to be drawn away by sin and evil, by faithlessness and godlessness, by money and pleasure, by egoism and impurity.

To the third angel there befalls the task of announcing the great chastisement: "anyone who worships the beast and its image, and accepts its mark on forehead or hand, will drink the wine of God's wrath, poured full strength into the cup of his terrible judgment, and will be tormented with fire and sulfur, in the presence of the Lamb and of the holy angels. The smoke of the fire that torments them never ends. Anyone who worships the beast and its image and whoever accepts the mark of its name has no relief day or nigh

At this final time of the great tribulation, announced as that of the end of the iniquity, of the defeat of Satan, and of the chastisement of the godless, the constancy of those who belong to the Lord, who put into practice the commandments of God and who remain faithful to Jesus, is put to a hard test.

For this reason, I urge you today to be particularly united with your guardian angels, in prayer, in harkening to their voice, and in accepting with docility their sure guidance, along the road of goodness and holiness.

In these stormy times, when Satan is ruling with all his dark power, the task of the angels of light of my Immaculate Heart is that of leading you all along the road of constancy and of fidelity to Jesus, in the observance of the commandments of God and in the practice of all the virtues.

Today, together with your guardian angels, I bless you with the joy of a Mother who is consoled and ever more glorified by you.

***

May 22, 1994, Feast of Pentecost:

Today you find yourself gathered together here, in a continuous cenacle of prayer with your heavenly Mother, in the liturgical celebration of the Solemnity of Pentecost.

And you are repeating, with the intensity of love, the prayer which I myself have taught you: "Come Holy Spirit, come by means of the powerful intercession of the Immaculate Heart of Mary, your well-beloved Spouse."

Come, Holy Spirit.

A new and universal effusion of the Holy Spirit is necessary to arrive at the new times, so longed for. It is necessary that the Second Pentecost come quickly. It can come to pass only in the spiritual cenacle of my Immaculate Heart. For this reason, I renew today the invitation to all the Church to enter into the cenacle which the heavenly Mother has prepared for you for the final times. You are able to enter through the act of consecration to my Immaculate Heart.

I request that this consecration, asked by me with such anxious insistence, be made by the bishops, the priests, the religious and the faithful. And let it be made by all in order to shorten the time of the great trial which has now arrived.

The Holy Spirit will then bring you to an understanding of the whole and entire truth.

The Holy Spirit will cause you to understand the times through which you are living.

The Holy Spirit will be light upon your way and will make you courageous witnesses of the Gospel in the dreadful hour of the great apostasy.

The Holy Spirit will bring you to grasp that which I will make manifest to you concerning what is contained in the still sealed Book.

The Holy Spirit will give his perfect witness to the Son, by preparing hearts and souls to receive Jesus who will return to you in glory.

Come, Holy Spirit.

Come by means of the powerful intercession of my Immaculate Heart. My hour is the hour of the Holy Spirit. The triumph of my Immaculate Heart will coincide with the great prodigy of the second Pentecost.

A NEW FIRE WILL COME DOWN FROM HEAVEN AND WILL PURIFY ALL HUMANITY, WHICH

HAS AGAIN BECOME PAGAN. IT WILL BE LIKE A JUDGMENT IN MINIATURE, AND EACH ONE WILL SEE HIMSELF IN THE LIGHT OF THE VERY TRUTH OF GOD.

THUS SINNERS WILL COME BACK TO GRACE AND HOLINESS; THE STRAYING, TO THE ROAD OF RIGHTEOUSNESS; THOSE FAR AWAY, TO THE HOUSE OF THE FATHER; THE SICK, TO COMPLETE HEALING; AND THE PROUD, THE IMPURE, THE WICKED COLLABORATORS WITH SATAN WILL BE DEFEATED AND CONDEMNED FOR EVER.

Then my motherly Heart will have its triumph over all humanity, which will return to a new marriage of love and of life with its Heavenly Father.

Come, Holy Spirit.

Come at the voice of your well-beloved Spouse who calls You. I am the heavenly Spouse of the Holy Spirit. As, through a singular design of the Father, I have become true Mother of the Son, so also have I become true Spouse of the Holy Spirit. The Holy Spirit has given Himself to my soul by an interior and true spousal union, and of this has been born the divine fruit of the virginal conception of the Word in my most pure womb.

The Spirit cannot resist the voice of the Spouse who calls to Him. And so unite yourselves, each and all, to me, my little children, in invoking today the gift of the Holy Spirit. Let your supplication become the prayer of these last times. Let your prayer be habitual, repeated frequently by you, because it has been taught to you and is being passionately demanded of you by your heavenly Mother: "Come, Holy Spirit, come by means of the powerful intercession of the Immaculate Heart of Mary, your well-beloved Spouse."

And open your hearts to hope, because there is about to come upon you the greatest prodigy of the second Pentecost.

***

June 4, 1995, Feast of Pentecost:

Gather together in an extraordinary cenacle of prayer made with me, beloved children, you are celebrating today the Solemnity of Pentecost.

I found myself gathered together with the apostles and disciples, in the Cenacle of Jerusalem, when the miracle of the descent of the Holy Spirit took place, under the form of tongues of fire. And I saw with joy the miracle of their complete transformation. Timid and fearful as they had been, they came forth from the Cenacle courageous and intrepid witnesses of Jesus and of his Gospel.

In the spiritual cenacle of my Immaculate Heart, the miraculous event of the Second Pentecost must now be accomplished, implored and expected by you. Again there will descend upon the Church and upon all humanity miraculous tongues of fire

Tongues of divine fire will bring heat and life to a humanity which has now become cold from egotism and hatred, from violence and wars. Thus the parched earth will be opened to the breath of the Spirit of God, which will transform it into a new and wondrous garden in which the Most Holy Trinity will make its permanent dwelling place among you.

Tongues of fire will come down to enlighten and sanctify the Church, which is living through the dark hour of Calvary and being stricken in her pastors, wounded in the flock, abandoned and betrayed by her own, exposed to the impetuous wind of errors, pervaded with the loss of faith and with apostasy.

The divine fire of the Holy Spirit will heal her of every malady, will purify her of every stain and every infidelity, will clothe her again in new beauty, will cover her with his splendor, in such a way that she may be able to find again all her unity an holiness, and will thus give to the world her full, universal and perfect witness to Jesus.

TONGUES OF FIRE WILL COME DOWN UPON YOU ALL, MY POOR CHILDREN, SO ENSNARED AND SEDUCED BY SATAN AND BY ALL THE EVIL SPIRITS WHO, DURING THESE YEARS, HAVE ATTAINED THEIR GREATEST TRIUMPH. AND THUS, YOU WILL BE ILLUMINATED BY THIS DIVINE LIGHT, AND YOU WILL SEE YOUR OWN SELVES IN THE MIRROR OF THE TRUTH AND

THE HOLINESS OF GOD. IT WILL BE LIKE A JUDGMENT IN MINIATURE, WHICH WILL OPEN THE DOOR OF YOUR HEART TO RECEIVE THE GREAT GIFT OF DIVINE MERCY.

And then the Holy Spirit will work the new miracle of universal transformation in the heart and the life of all: sinners will be converted; the weak will find support; the sick will receive healing; those far away will return to the house of the Father; those separated and divided will attain full unity.

In this way, the miracle of the second Pentecost will take place. It will come with the triumph of my Immaculate Heart in the world.

Only then will you see how the tongues of fire of the Spirit of Love will renew the whole world, which will become completely transformed by the greatest manifestation of divine mercy.

And so, I invite you to spend this day in the cenacle, gathered together in prayer with me, Mother of Mercy, in the hope and trembling expectation of the second Pentecost, now close at hand.

***

<u>May 26, 1996:</u>

With an extraordinary cenacle of prayer and fraternity, you celebrate today the solemnity of Pentecost. You recall the prodigious event of the

descent of the Holy Spirit, under the form of tongues of fire, upon the Cenacle of Jerusalem, where the Apostles were gathered in prayer, with me, your heavenly Mother.

You, too, gathered today in prayer in the spiritual cenacle of my Immaculate Heart, prepare yourselves to receive the prodigious gift of the second Pentecost.

The second Pentecost will come to bring this humanity which has again become pagan and which is living under the power influence of the Evil One—back to its full communion of life with its Lord who has created, redeemed and saved it.

MIRACULOUS AND SPIRITUAL TONGUES OF FIRE WILL PURIFY THE HEARTS AND THE SOULS OF ALL, WHO WILL SEE THEMSELVES IN THE LIGHT OF GOD AND WILL BE PIERCED BY THE KEEN SWORD OF HIS DIVINE TRUTH.

The second Pentecost will come to lead all the Church to the summit of her greatest splendor. The Spirit of Wisdom will lead her to perfect fidelity to the Gospel the Spirit of Counsel will assist her and comfort her in all their tribulations; the Spirit of Fortitude will bring her to a daily and heroic witness to Jesus. Above all, the Holy Spirit will communicate to the Church the precious gift of her full unity and of her greatest holiness. Only then will Jesus bring into her his reign of glory.

The Second Pentecost will descend into hearts to transform them and make them sensitive and open to love, humble and merciful, free of all egoism and of all wickedness. And thus it will be that the Spirit of the Lord will transform the hearts of stone into hearts of flesh.

The second Pentecost will burn away, with the fire of his divine love, the sins which obscure the beauty of your souls. And thus, they will return to the full communion of life with God; they will be a privileged garden of his presence; and in the resplendent garden there will blossom all the virtues, cultivated with special care by me, your heavenly Gardener. Thus the Holy Spirit will pour out upon the earth the gift of his divine holiness.

The second Pentecost will descend upon all the nations which are so divided by egoism and particular interests, by antagonisms which often set them one against the other. And thus are spread everywhere the wars and fratricidal struggles which have caused so much blood to be spilt on your streets. Then, the nations will form part of one single great family, gathered together and blessed by the presence of the Lord among you.

Today I invite you to enter into the cenacle of my Immaculate Heart, to recollect yourselves in prayer with me, your heavenly Mother. And thus, together let us await the descent of the second Pentecost, which will renew the world and change the face of the earth.

"The Mini-Judgment is a reality. People no longer realize that they offend Me."

-God the Father to Matthew Kelly

Matthew Kelly

CHAPTER TEN

MATTHEW KELLY

"The Lord roars from on high, from his holy dwelling he raises his voice; Mightily he roars over the range, a shout like that of vintagers over the grapes. To all who inhabit the earth to its very ends the uproar spreads; For the Lord has an indictment against the nations, He is to pass judgment on all mankind."

— Jer. 25: 30-31

Born in Sydney, Australia, Matthew Kelly grew up in a large family of eight brothers, of which he was the fourth. His mother, Jenny, managed the home while his father, Bernard, supplied catering equipment to restaurants and bakeries. By 1993, Matthew was on a path to success. He studied commerce and majored in marketing at the University of Western Sydney. He enjoyed sports and music. He liked all the things people his age everywhere like. Thus, perhaps it is revealing that on that first night, the voice he heard intervened only after Matthew reluctantly removed the radio headset from his head.

It all began that night with a feeling, an intense feeling. Matthew says he had planned to listen to music before falling asleep, but moments after putting on his headphones, a strong sensation overcame him. It was an uncontrollable urge. After a few moments, he fell to his knees in prayer by his bed. It was something he wasn't prone to do. Then, as he knelt in the darkness slightly before midnight, the feeling intensified. Suddenly, he says, there was a voice, a very clear voice. Even though it wasn't audible, Matthew remembers that he could "hear" it: **"Keep doing what you are doing and believe in yourself and in Me."**

With that, the incident ended. The voice said no more, and the urgent feeling disappeared. The next morning, Matthew was not sure what had happened. However, something started to erase his anxiety. It was a "peace," he says. "A tremendous peace had filled me at that moment, and it remained with me," he said. The supernatural events in Matthew Kelly's life began during Holy Week. Four days later, on Easter Sunday, April 11, 1993, something happened while he was at Mass. At the moment of the consecration of the bread and wine, he says the voice spoke to him again. **"Listen to Me, hear My words, and do My will."**

This time, Kelly says, he knew the voice was real beyond a doubt. And he understood the events of the first night had been genuine. Two days later, the voice revealed its identity: **"I am your Heavenly Father."** After that, Matthew Kelly's life would never be the same. He began to receive locutions and messages from the Eternal Father, an extraordinary number of them, sometimes ten a day.

In Australia, on June 5, 1993, the Eternal Father reportedly gave him the following message concerning "a mini-judgment." Perhaps as much as any previous message, it tells us how God views this coming supernatural event:

> **The mini-judgment is a reality. People no longer realize that they offend Me. Out of My infinite Mercy I will provide a mini-judgment. It will be painful, very painful, but short. You will see your sins, you will see how much you offend Me every day. I know that you think this sounds like a very good thing, but unfortunately, even this won't bring the whole world into My love. Some people will turn even further away from Me, they will be proud and stubborn.**

Satan is working hard against Me.

Poor souls, all of you, robbed of the knowledge of My love. Be ready for this "judgment" of Mine. Judgment is the best word you humans have to describe it, but it will be more like this: you will see your own personal darkness contrasted against the pure light of My love.

Those who repent will be given an unquenchable thirst for this light. Their love for Me then will be so strong that, united with Mary's Immaculate Heart and the Sacred heart of Jesus, the head of Satan shall be crushed and he will be detained in Hell forever. All those who love Me will join to help form the heel that crushes Satan. Then as you all die naturally, your thirst for this light will be quenched, you shall see Me your God. You shall live in My love, you will be in Heaven. Now do you see how important these times are? Don't wait for this mini-judgment, you must start to look at yourselves more closely so that you can see your faults and repent. Your are fortunate to have the faith needed to read, believe and accept this message. You must not go away indifferent to it. You must examine yourself more every day and pray in reparation.

All of you, be like the blind man. Each day you should cry, "Lord, open my eyes," and My Son will open your eyes so that you can see your wretchedness and repent. Pray now more than ever and remember the world's standards are a false indication of My Justice. I am your God, and while I am perfectly merciful to those who repent, I am perfectly just to those who do not. Many people think that I, your God, won't mind, it's only little, they say. But it's not a matter of minding. I want people to love Me. Love respects little things as well as the big things and in the most case these little things are not so little.

Do not judge your actions, or other's actions. You are unable to judge, you are incapable of judging, because you cannot read a man's heart. You must love Me with your whole heart, with your whole mind, with your whole soul and with your whole strength. Today is the day. Do your best to renounce yourself and let Christ reign in your lives. You will never be ready for the mini-judgment, but some will be more prepared than others. You must aim to be one of those and bring as many others as you can to be prepared or as prepared as possible. Above all do not fear. I don't tell you all this to become scared. No, simply try to become better people each day, more than this I could not ask. I am your God, I am perfectly just and perfectly merciful. You are sons and daughters of Mine. Does not a father look after his children? I send this message to spare you from any pain I can, but the pain that you experience by seeing the darkness of your souls is an act of love on My behalf. Do you not see that this will return many, many souls to a fuller love of Me? This will save many souls from the fires of Hell. This is the most important of all My messages: I am the Lord your God, you are My sons and daughters whom I love very much, and My greatest delight is in being with you, and I want to be with you for eternity. Anything I do is done out of love for you, My children. Trust in Me, your Heavenly Father.

CHAPTER ELEVEN

A PREVIEW OF THE ILLUMINATION: SOULS WHO HAVE EXPERIENCED JUDGMENT

"I tell you, on the day of judgment people will render an account for every careless word they speak."

— Mt 12:36

The conversion of Saint Paul on the road to Damascus has often been given as an illustration of what this miraculous event, the illumination of all consciences, may be like. As Scripture tells us, the fiercely anti-Christian Saul experienced a glorious vision and was penetrated by a powerful light that converted him of his sin. Saint Paul, they say, responded to this illumination and repented. These writers point out that the illumination of his soul was a grace that he could have rejected, yet he went on to become a great saint.

In addition to his conscience becoming aware of God's will for him, it appears Saint Paul experienced, to some degree, an infused revelation of Christian truth. Scripture says Paul began to preach that Jesus was the "Son of God" just "days" after his conversion, indicating he became very knowledgeable, almost instantaneously, of the teachings of Christianity. But although the illumination of one's conscience may indirectly have this effect on some, an enlightenment of conscience is not to be confused with a revelation of Christian truth. While souls after this miraculous event may be able to search and find truth in Christianity, evangelization will remain the primary mode of bringing to all the Gospel of Jesus Christ. Private revelation confirms this fact, as a great evangelization is foretold to come. Likewise, the Pope often mentions such a coming time in the world for Christians. The illumination of conscience, then, will not be a revelation of Christian truth, as Saint Paul may have experienced along with his illumination, but certainly a stepping stone in that direction.

In our century, there appears to be some chosen souls, like St. Paul, who God has clearly given what one may call a foreshadowing experience of the coming illumination of conscience. On December 18, 1924, a noted French priest, Fr. John Lamy (1855-1931), known as Perè Lamy, reported a mystical experience in which he was shown "by a light" his soul and all of his shortcomings. This occurred as he was in adoration before the Blessed Sacrament:

> Immediately I saw about the Host, exposed above the high altar, a wonderful radiance of light. This radiance took complete possession of my field of vision. Far more luminous in every way than the sun, it left only the Blessed Sacrament visible. Whether my eyes were open or shut, it did not vary in any way. And moreover, I saw in this light all my soul with its qualities and its defects, as though it were behind me. (December 18, 1924)

The recently cannonized Polish mystic, Saint Faustina Kowalska (1905-1938) also reported a spiritual encounter with the Lord that allowed her to see the state of her soul as God saw it:

> Once I was summoned to the judgment (seat) of

God. I stood alone before the Lord. Jesus appeared such as we know Him during His Passion. After a moment, His wounds disappeared except for five, those in His hands, His feet and His side. Suddenly I saw the complete condition of my soul as God sees it. I could clearly see all that is displeasing to God. I did not know that even the smallest transgressions will have to be accounted for.

What a moment! Who can describe it? To stand before the Thrice-Holy God! Jesus asked me, **"Who are you?"** I answered, "I am Your servant Lord." **"You are guilty of one day of fire in purgatory."** I wanted to throw myself immediately into the flames of purgatory, but Jesus stopped me and said, **"Which do you prefer, suffer now for one day in purgatory or for a short while on earth?"** I replied, "Jesus, I want to suffer in purgatory, and I want to suffer also the greatest pains on earth, even if it were until the end of the world."

Jesus said: **"One [of the two] is enough; you will go back to earth, and there you will suffer much, but not for long; you will accomplish My will and My desires, and a faithful servant of Mine will help you to do this. Now, rest you head on My bosom, on My heart, and draw from it strength and power for these sufferings, because you will find neither relief nor help nor comfort anywhere else. Know that you will have much, much to suffer, but don't let this frighten you; I am with you."**

Saint Faustina's life and writings were silenced by the Church for over twenty years. The diary of Saint Faustina, *Divine Mercy in My Soul,* is considered a spiritual classic today. Pope John Paul II initiated the reinvestigation of her life and writings while he was Archbishop of Cracow. She was declared Blessed in April of 1993 and canonized on April 30, 2000.

Because Saint Faustina was canonized in the year 2000, some believe that if the miracle takes place this same year (2000), it would be the ultimate approbation of her message of Divine Mercy in our time. This is because the miracle is prophesied to be the greatest act of Divine Mercy.

There are more personal accounts of souls experiencing "a judgment." Since 1985, several individuals have gone on record as having received such an awareness, either through an experience or a dream. From their accounts, these individuals especially note how they were shown how "all" sin offends God and how God judges every little thought, word and deed.

St. Faustina Kowalska

CHAPTER TWELVE

FR. STEPHEN SCHEIER

"A wise son loves correction, but the senseless one heeds no rebuke."

— Prv 13:1

In 1985, Fr Stephen Scheier, a Catholic priest, was involved in a head-on collision with a truck. Unconscious, he found himself before the Judgment Seat of God:

> I was before the judgment seat of Our Lord. I did not see Him. There was much said in regards to my life. The only thing that I did when I heard about particular instances, was internally say, "Yes...Yes— that's true." There was no rebuttal. At the end of His speaking, God said, **"The sentence that you will have for all eternity is Hell."** I thought internally, "I know—this is what I deserve." At that moment, I heard a female voice. The voice said, **"Son, would You please spare his life."** Our Lord then said, **"Mother—he has been a priest for twelve years for himself and not for Me...Let Him reap the punishment he deserves."** At that, I heard her say again in response, **"But Son, if we give to him special graces and strengths, and come to him in ways that he is not familiar with, we can see if he bears fruit... If he does not, then Your will be done."** There was a very short pause. And the Lord

said, **"Mother he's yours."**

Fr. Scheier recalls that, indeed, he deserved to go to Hell, for he had not fulfilled his duty as a priest:

> I could not stand peer pressure. In other words, I wanted to be one of the guys. Now the priests at this time seemed to find a need to be just one of the guys, too—a lay person. And that was shone more from the pulpit than any place else in my dealings with priests and laity —because priests would get up and talk about peace, love and joy— not morality, dogma, and what the Church is all about—because this made one unpopular and God help us if a priest was unpopular. Because that would mean that the money didn't come in. So to keep the money coming in you had to tell the people what they wanted to hear.

Needless to say, Fr. Scheier is a very changed man today. Appearing on many programs throughout the country, he travels where ever invited to tell his story and to convey this reality to all who will listen.

Fr. Stephen Scheier

CHAPTER THIRTEEN

CHRISTOPHER WINTERS

"A king seated on the throne of judgment dispels all evil with his glance."

— Prv 20:8

Christopher Winters is a 45 year-old photo-journalist living in Cranberry, Pennsylvania. In 1988, he too had a life-changing experience in which he "experienced a Judgment" of his soul:

> Church was not a priority in my life. I wasn't anti-Church or angry or bitter from some past, difficult experience with the Church. I just didn't go on Sunday. I suppose I was like many young people; building a family and a career and not necessarily concerned about God and His role in my life. It just wasn't an issue.
>
> But a friend of mine had noticed that I enjoyed people's stories when I produced programs. I like to hear the experiences of their lives which put them in the place and frame of mind that they now hold. He asked me to visit a shrine in Western Maryland called the National Shrine Grotto of Lourdes. The suggestion didn't go over real well with me. I remember saying, "Why do I need that religious stuff in my life?" He was patient, but persistent, and just kept politely inviting me to go to see this place and the Monsignor who runs

it. This went on for a period of months. Finally I relented as a way of appeasing him and hoping that a visit to the shrine would end his requests once and for all.

The Shrine is dedicated to the Virgin Mary. Of all the people in the Bible, I probably knew the least about her. I knew of her, but I didn't know her. How could I possibly do a story or a program about a woman I did not know.

When I arrived at the Shrine, the Monsignor said "I think you're an answer to prayer. I have been praying for someone to do a video about this place, and asked the Blessed Mother to send someone." The thought startled me. I said "Monsignor, I don't think I'm your guy." He said "Why not?" I replied "Because I know that Mary is the Mother of God, but I don't know anything more about her. And I would not wish to do her story poorly." He just paused, then smiled at me and said, "You're perfect for this." I said "I don't think so, Monsignor. It's a beautiful place, but I think there are others more qualified to do this story." He said, "Are you uncomfortable being here?" I said, "No, I just haven't been close to the Church, so I'm probably not where I need to be spiritually in order to do this tape." He said, "Are you angry with the Church?" And I said "No, it isn't anger. Probably just apathy and laziness more than anything else."

And he looked at me for a moment and then said "That's fair enough. I'll make you a deal. Why don't you just go up into the Grotto and kneel down in the little chapel up there. That's where Mother Seton used to pray. Don't try to remember your formal prayers, just say whatever is in your heart. When you're done, come back to me. If you still feel the same way, I'll give you my blessing and you can go on your way. No hard feelings." I figured that was my way out. I said, "Fine," and proceeded into the Grotto.

It was evening and late summer heading into fall. There were the evening sounds of the insects and birds and such as they were ending their day. I particularly remember the sound of locusts making their loud, rhythmic buzzing as the sun was drawing low on the horizon. I think I was the only person in the shrine that evening, at least as far as I could tell, because it was getting close to closing time. I saw no one else inside the shrine as I slowly headed for the chapel.

Born and raised Catholic, many of the symbols of the Church were coming back to me on my slow trek into the Grotto. But I had fallen away and had probably not been to Mass for ten years or better.

There was a distinct, powerful sense of peace inside the Grotto. It was very relaxing and almost comforting. The grounds were beautiful, the smells were fantastic and it seemed as if all of my senses were more alert than usual.

The chapel itself was small, much like the old-style one room school houses. But it was made of stone and rimmed with vibrant stained glass windows. There were only a few pews in there, and it was obvious this was a prayer chapel and not a chapel for a full Mass. There simply wouldn't be enough room to put more than 15 to 20 people inside. At the center of the Chapel was a Tabernacle and behind it a statue of the Virgin Mary as the Queen of Heaven and she was holding the infant Jesus.

I knelt down and began to think about my life and my relationship with God. I wasn't close to Him. I believed there was "something" out there somewhere, but didn't know if it was Jesus, Buddah, Muhammad, whoever. Was any one religion right? Were they all partially correct and nobody had a monopoly on God? Was He even called "God" or some other name?

At that point in my life I was having trouble with a business partner and difficulties in my marriage. I started thinking about those things. I started thinking about my poor heath and how I was in emergency rooms on a regular basis, as often as 2-3 times per week. And then I read something on the plaque beneath the crucifix. Part of what it said was "You are now in front of the Lord God of all Creation. What would you say to Him?"

For some reason that question floored me. If there really was One God, and only One God, and I could say one thing...just one thing...what would I say?

I started making a "wish list" in my head of things I wanted from God. For my family, for my business, for myself. I started clicking them off one by one and almost wishing out loud for these things. But then I stopped and said, "No." I leaned back up to the crucifix and I said, "If I could say one thing and only one thing to the Lord God of all of Creation, by whatever name He is known, I would just say,

'Thanks.'" Thanks for allowing me to be. I'll take the good with the bad. Thank you for allowing me to ever be at all.

At the time, I was not one given to prayer. I prayed more to the ceiling or to the sky or to "someone" but not to an individual who I really believed was there. I didn't know if I was being heard of not. Sometimes it felt as if my prayers were futile and useless because they often seemed to go unanswered or even acknowledged. This time was different.

There was no peel of thunder or flash of lighting. But suddenly there was a beautiful fragrance in the chapel. Being late in the year, I though this was odd and reminded myself to ask the Monsignor what flowers made such a beautiful fragrance and still were in bloom at this time of year.

Suddenly, I was aware of a presence in front of me about an arm's length away or slightly further and to my right of the Tabernacle. I knew exactly where this person was, but didn't see anybody. I couldn't even tell if it was a man or a woman. But it was a little "somebody." That much I could tell. Nothing was said. Since this presence was small and seemingly harmless, I wasn't afraid and didn't mind if he/she wished to stay. It was pretty in there, the smells were terrific, and I was relaxed and peaceful.

After a short pause, all of the bugs and birds ceased their noise at exactly the same time. I was still awake, still alert. But the noise stopped instantly, as if on command. Now it was dead quiet in there. And it seemed more as if it were a respectful quiet than a hush for the evening. Then there was another presence in front of me, this on the other side of the Tabernacle and this one had power, Authority. And it was a man. And he began to look not at me, but through me. I said nothing. And then he began to call to mind every decision I had ever made in my life and was reviewing them with me through his eyes. All of it was happening at a blinding speed, but I could recall in perfect and clear detail every decision and every conversation from years ago, some of them long ago forgotten. He was calling to something inside of me and it was answering him. I was simply a spectator on this journey watching the same things he was watching and seeing them through his eyes, not mine. And I began to realize that this was truly the Lord God of All of Creation and He was going to make a "judgment" about me when He was finished. I also realized His decision would be permanent, without appeal, and forever.

This look at my life and my decisions pointed out a few things to me right away. In looking at my life through his eyes, I was not being condemned or ridiculed. The process was terrible to have to endure and I am quite certain that it would kill many. It was that horrific. But not because of condemnation or accusation on his part, just the horror of seeing the pattern of a life of decisions and how they were so far from where they needed to be in order to gain eternal life.

I was failing this test miserably. I was not going to make it to Heaven. He was going to throw me out and I agreed with his assessment.

In watching His review, I began to see things in a

different way. By looking with His eyes, I saw how much I had offended Him, even in the tiniest of ways. The things which were being held up in front of me were sometimes so very small. I began to cry with a heartfelt sorrow. I was seeing me as God sees me and I didn't like what I saw. And I said, *"My Lord, I am sorry."* And I meant it from the bottom of my heart. At that moment the review stopped. And there was a pause as He stopped to consider my fate. And I knew this would be forever. Then He spoke one sentence and only one sentence. He said, **"My dear Child, your sins I shall remember no more."** And they were gone. Divine Forgiveness. I felt it happen and I physically felt different. Cleaner. Lighter. Much, much different.

I can honestly say that there was a most incredible sense of peace and calm throughout this process. As difficult as it was to watch, there was not fear. There was a tremendous sense of endless and uncondi- tional love which had been around from the beginning of time and had waited to give back this love to anyone wishing to receive it. Many have called what I experienced, "The Warning" discussed by the children of Garabandal. I don't know if I would call it a warning. Perhaps. If you are not in the right frame of mind with God, it would be a warning. But I felt as if it was one of the finest gifts I have ever received from God. All of my questions about Him and where I stood with Him were gone. I felt love like I never thought possible and a tremendous, deep, deep peace. I slept like I have never slept before on the night that this happened.

I got up to leave from the chapel in a much different

state. I was elated and surprised at the same time. Everyone of my senses seemed more alert than usual. I turned to leave the Grotto and go back out of the shrine to my car.

As I got about half way out of the shrine, I realized I was no longer able to move. I had stopped. But I wasn't grabbed or anything, I just wasn't moving anymore. And then I heard two sentences. The first was **"be not afraid."** The second was **"prepare ye the way of the Lord."**

With that two sensations started at the same time. First there was a powerful sensation in the bottom of my feet much like an electrical charge. Sort of like the feeling you get when you ding your funnybone, only this didn't hurt but it was extremely powerful. It began in the bottom of my feet and was working its way all the way up through me. And I could tell it was healing me and "fixing" me as it went.

The second was an immediate rush of Scripture flowing through my head at lightening speed. It was flying through me. It began with the Old Testament and went on through the New Testament and the Book of Revelation. There was nothing new here. But suddenly it all made sense. It was a repetition of the same truth over and over again. A timeless and eternal Truth. But since there was no longer sin upon me, I could see it clearly for the first time. And it was such a beautiful revelation. The love wrapped around the power of these words was enough to bring tears of joy to my eyes. Most of the Scriptural passages dealt with the fire of the Holy Spirit. And until that point, I had always felt that the words "Holy Spirit" were a metaphor, like saying "the spirit of the law," not a real person. I was wrong. Because this was Him.

But I also realized this was the same fire which once destroyed Sodom and Gomorrah. The same fire upon a burning bush which spoke to Moses. The same fire which came to rest upon the Apostles at Pentecost. And it was now upon me.

There was a distinct personality to this fire. Separate from me, but working in conjunction with me. I could see and hear its thoughts and emotions, work through it under the authority of God, but not control it. It wasn't mine. There was a beautiful peace, and almost a playfulness about this Spirit. It feared nothing. It was the controlling force of all creation. And it was now upon me like a blanket or a coat of armor. I felt very protected.

As the Scriptures ended, so did the feeling of electricity in my body. They stopped at the same time. And when they were finished, there was left behind the presence of the Holy Spirit. And He said one sentence. He said **"You shall travel the world telling the story of the Blessed Virgin."** Until a few moments earlier, I did not know the story of the Blessed Virgin. Now I did.

I started a video production company dedicated to the Blessed Virgin and the Lord Jesus Christ. That company, either myself or people I have hired to work with me, has now been in some twenty foreign countries all over the world telling the story of the Blessed Virgin. And it feels like we have so much more yet to do.

After that day, there began a series of "teachings" about Scripture which lasted for a period of several months. He (the Holy Spirit) taught me about what God was saying through the Scriptures, how He wanted to be followed, how much He had in store for us, how very, very much He loves us.

But there were more difficult words, too. Words like Chastisement and Purification. They must come. It must happen. And it will. But the world has been granted a time to prepare and change. That time is now upon us.

Within a short time of my experiences at the Grotto, all of my children were baptized. We started going to Church again. And I started praying the Rosary, a prayer I never even recited as a child. I didn't know why this was important to me, but it became a burning desire in me. And I felt that terrific peace again when I did pray my Rosary prayers. They were also a source of tremendous insight and inspiration during my many meditations.

There is so much more to tell and I feel as if I have only lightly scratched the surface. I wish I could explain in great detail the prophecies I have literally watched fulfilled in front of me and how I have seen the laws of nature stopped in front of my own eyes. The impossible has become almost routine. It has been quite an experience.

And all the while, even through the toughest of times, a new sense of peace and love. I would only repeat the words of the Angel to those who wonder about

God: **"Be not afraid."**

I have since come to the realization that all of us will ultimately face this "judgment" at some point. I happened to have a miniature version of mine in this lifetime while I still have time to make changes. Others will face this at a time when they do not have an opportunity to change. Then it will be too late.

Why this experience happened, I'm not sure. But it taught me that we are all called to be good examples in this lifetime and every day is an opportunity to fulfill that calling. Take time to make friends. Say "please" and "thank you." Appreciate the little courtesies and overlook the offenses. Be grateful that God ever permitted you to be at all.

In my teachings, I have learned a great deal of what is to come, some of which I cannot say now. But if we do what the Virgin Mary has said of us to do in her many apparitions, the rightful Judgment of God will be spared. If not, it will come and very, very few will survive. And they, too, will agree with God's decision.

"My dear child, Your sins I shall remember no more."

National Shrine Grotto of Lourdes

"I also understood that they were being shown how they offended God and how this hurt God."

-Dr. Frank Novasack, Jr.

Dr. Frank Novasack, Jr.

CHAPTER FOURTEEN

DR. FRANK NOVASACK, JR.

"Your commandment we have not heeded or observed, nor have we done as you ordered as for our good, Therefore all you have brought upon us, all you have done to us, you have done by a proper judgment."

— Dan 3:30-31

D r. Frank Novasack Jr. is a 46 year-old doctor practicing in Pittsburgh, Pennsylvania. On December 31, 1999, he received a powerful dream, a dream that found him descending into a subterranean location where he witnessed, participated in, and felt a "Judgment" occurring:

> In my dream I felt as though I was close to death and a coming judgment, and I sensed I was traveling to the place of judgment. There were others with me. Everyone else was not taking anything with them, but I felt compelled to pack enough clothes for a period. I sensed that I was going to either Purgatory or to Hell, and I feared that it was possibly Hell. Also accompanying me were two men from my past, who I remembered had personal problems in college.
>
> I soon found myself getting on an elevator with two large suitcases and then going down many floors. The elevator descended many levels and suddenly

I realized that I was possibly getting close to Hell. I became very frightened about where I was going. Finally, I got off the elevator and I walked down a long corridor that resembled an underground airport shuttle. I then went down another series of elevators, and was again scared that I was about to face Hell.

Finally, I arrived in this big underground conference auditorium that had a large audience of people in it. There was a lot of noise going on. On a stage like platform, like a judge's bench, there were people speaking who were talking about morality and ethics. Simultaneously, there were also speakers with microphones in the audience, addressing the people at the different, higher levels in front.

As I watched I realized that it appeared that a judgment of some kind was occurring, and that there was a great level of suffering being experienced by the people in the audience. I noticed the people were suffering mentally upon the realization of the sins that they had committed, more than anything else. I also understood that they were being shown how they had offended God and how this hurt God.

I then noticed a young lady, who was maybe in her late 20's in age, being lectured to about her sin. Once again, I felt a keen, almost painful awareness of sin and the mental grief which outweighed any physical suffering over the offense towards God. The speaker addressed this young lady about her alcoholism and how it had led her into further sin. But she was in denial and yelled back to the speaker that it wasn't that bad and that she didn't feel like she's done anything wrong. "I didn't do anything so bad...I didn't do anything so bad," I heard her say.

A floor-lamp light in an aisle was shining in my eyes and I went to adjust it to shine at a different angle. As I adjusted the light slightly, it caused several people to instantly disappear. I was then sternly warned by one of the speakers on the stage or bench area, not to touch any of the lights and not to "alter the lighting." The "lighting," he said, "could influence major changes."

As the "judgment" continued, I continued to watch. I eventually woke up in a panic, quite shocked by the dream. I was shaken for days after this and still remember it very clearly. From it all, I was left with a deep understanding of how our smallest sins offend God and how intense the psychological and emotional component of our "judgment" will perhaps be. I also felt I was made aware of how this all is related to "the act of contrition" that we say during confession.

*The Illumination will be a miracle of healing
and restoration through the Father.*

CHAPTER FIFTEEN

A DEEPER UNDERSTANDING

"Sing a new song to the Lord who has done marvelous deeds, whose right hand and holy arm have won the victory. The Lord has made his victory known, has revealed his triumph for the nations to see, has remembered faithful love, toward the House of Israel. All the ends of the earth have seen the victory of our God."

— Ps 98-1:2

God has revealed certain insights concerning why the miracle must come now and what this "awakening" will truly mean for the world and all of His children:

1)   The miracle of conscience is being given to the world because the reason Christ was sent by the Father has been, for the most part, forgotten. Therefore, the Illumination will begin, in a dramatic fashion, the almost instantaneous realization that God exists.

2)   The ungodly culture of our time has caused many innocent victims great suffering. Innocent and vulnerable, these are God's children, and He wishes to end their suffering and to bring them home to their rightful inheritance—now.

3)   Satan's ferocity and evil are at an all time intensity and this is causing the downfall of many soul—souls not designed for the culture of Satan and who are living outside of the will

of God. But Jesus is near them. They are not forgotten, and through the transformation the miracle will bring, their lives will be lifted up and brought back home to the Father. This will occur because of God's great love for His people.

4) The time has come for God's great victory, long promised. Mankind must be transformed, and part of the answer to the millions of prayers over the centuries is this "miracle of transformation." It will be in a special way, a triumph of the Rosary.

5) The great transformation that will occur from the Illumination will be unlike any religious transformation before, for it will come totally from "within" not without. Indeed, it will come from deep within hearts, which will be ready after living through so much dysfunction in the decadence of our culture and after so much preparation by Mary, our Mother. To a degree, God has always come from within, but He will now, in an even greater way, through the Illumination. All this can be seen as a medicine, a cure showered upon the earth. The earth is in a dense virus-like fog and now will come the cure. But like many cures, it will be uncomfortable and painful for some. Such will be the moment of truth for these souls.

6) In a mystical way, after the miracle, all that is present will become new. All will be transformed by God. Those who are in confusion need not be afraid, for come the impact of the Illumination, all that is of God will be drawn to Him from the disarray.

7) Each person's heart who comes back to God will be like a temple purified, for God desires change and this will be His *"call"* for His children's attention. The Illumination will be His clapping hands, causing alarm and surprise so all will

stop and listen. There will be no other invitation after this, the chosen ones tell us. It is a rhapsody to be played out, with prayer calling the love of children to the love of their Father. God's voice will bellow through the clouds, mankind's ears will cock and listen. Looking to the heavens in attention, God desires none of His children at this time to be lost. He wants His voice, through the Illumination, to be heard.

8) It is God's strength, not man's, that will make the difficult road for some easier. Coming back to God now, in our times of materialism, sexuality, and paganism, will not be an easy road to haul for many. But God's strength will permit the transformation of many hearts to take place. He will be with us, healing His children, providing for their needs. He is the Lord Our God, and we will feel His presence. He will pass through us, and be in us, as our hearts will communicate the rhythm and harmony of His desired will. And for those not strong enough, He will wipe away all tears, taking souls unto Himself and then keeping them out of harm's way.

9) The Illumination will be a true awakening—a renewal. It will place mankind back on course, and will, for the first time, give mankind a true understanding of its Heavenly Father. For too long we have often known Him as an old man. He is far from such a concept. He is life—strong and vital, and the Illumination will reveal this to the world.

10) The Illumination will reveal the *"effects"* of the choices generations of people have made through disordered passion, a long sojourn outside of God's will. Indeed, the effects of sin have mutated the destiny of many. Thus, the illumination of conscience will wed Heaven and earth, bypassing the generations of damage, the hurdles Satan

created in man's journey home.

11)   From the Illumination will follow a new blueprint for the Church in its march through salvation history. A new path will emerge, the path home, ushering in a new oneness with the Father, Jesus, and the Holy Spirit on earth. A new process of thinking will emerge, man will come to see the Creator in all things. This *"divine spark"* will touch the faithful in such a way that many miracles will happen. Trust and love of God will imprint itself on souls and God's sheep will know green pastures.

12)   A new unity amongst Christians will come from the Illumination, for all Christians will seek to embrace God's will in a special way—and Christ's will *is* unity. All Christians will be invited into the house of the Father. There they will stop and listen and spend time with Him, away from misleading ideas and distractions. The Church will be one, a family, and much healing will come.

13)   After the Illumination, God will dwell in His *"special"* souls in a new way. Those consecrated to the Father will follow Him and honor Him, a perfect harmony will emerge through the Holy Spirit, and their lives will be transformed.

14)   The Illumination will serve as a link, a bridge between a time before the storm and a time after. It will serve as a call to shelter, for the world needs a great purifying to revive and cleanse it, something which Christ has also promised will come after His "warning." Indeed, a purifying fire will sweep across the land refining and cleansing, so that all that is good and pure will begin anew, all that is not will be razed.

15)   New times and new traditions will come after the

Illumination. The Church, consumed by God's love, will be shown how to complete it's mission.

16) The great miracle of conscience will allow all to *"feel"* God's power. This in turn will bring God's children that are in darkness into the light—those who never recognized the darkness before and, therefore, didn't notice the light. But soon, these souls will "see" and will gather around the Lord. Those still choosing to remain in the dark will have a very difficult time, if not impossible, returning home. But every effort will be made to save these souls. The great Illumination will be like a ladder for them. One step at a time, many will eventually come into the light. Christ will especially fight for these poor souls during the upheaval, even to the extent of taking extreme measures to prove His love for all His children.

17) The "Illumination" will be like a *"call"* from the Father, who sees His children unable to find their way home in the darkness without needing extreme measures of intervention. It will be like a fever racing across the earth. Trust, hope, and love will be rooted up from the hearts of God's people. All of this being the will and plan of God in giving "Illumination" to the world.

18) Those who respond to the grace of the miracle will find a treasure within themselves, a deep holy place they did not know existed. The Illumination will be like a fountain of water, washing souls clean, revealing what was buried under so much debris. Because of all of Mary's work, God is aware that the world at this time is like a tree with ripe fruit. After the miracle, the fruit will be able to be picked.

19) For those who say no to the "Illumination," there will be great anguish and many will be left blind. Hard-hearted

souls will have received great graces—but to no avail. Thus, they will be in the throes of eternal death. But for those who respond—they will be on the road home to their Father. Their hearts excised of hardness, their coldness melted—ready to be absorbed and subsumed into God. A bond between the creatures and the Creator will be possible—a bond of love, for God's children will have new hearts.

20)   The Illumination will be a separating process. Those who have eyes and ears to see and hear will be drawn to a new life. It will be like the polarization of a magnet. But those not drawn, will have to be destroyed in order to prevent re-contamination. Thus, the purification much come.

21)   After the Illumination, many souls will, upon seeing their state, feel uncertain of the grace they received. The love of the Father will be a great re-awakening. It will be the fulfillment of the prophecy of Isaiah: "A time will come when hearts will be opened up to the Lord...prior to my coming." Indeed, God's "kiss" from the heavens will open the hearts of His children.

22)   The Illumination will demand a "choice" in the hearts of all. People will still have to "choose" God, although He will be anxiously waiting for them. They will have to choose to come home. There will be no other time in history like it. God's sweet and tender mercy, wrapped around the fisted hand of His justice.

23)   The "Illumination" will call people to their rightful inheritance—a true dialogue with their God and Father. We are called to live in God and to invite Him to live in us. Thus, the purifying and transforming love of God will bring about such a change. Each child is unique in God's plan.

The Illumination will permit the fruition of God's plan in many of His children—simple hearts, now open to God's love.

24) Heaven and earth will touch through the miracle; they will intersect. Light and love will touch the earth, renewing its face. The Father will be present again, bringing the time of revelry to an end. Like a window that separates but doesn't, the Illumination will resonate a divine vibration into souls, a vibration of pure love which will stir the consciences of all, wiping the window clean so all can see the face of God.

25) After the Illumination, all that is not of God will not survive. Christ, through the Illumination, is coming to reclaim what is His. There will be no return to the ways of today, of our times. God's plan will be accomplished in full. What doesn't come home, will be left out in the cold, forever lost.

26) The plan, Mary's plan of peace, will be fulfilled in stages, not to be overshadowed by the rotting, evil remnants of a bygone time—a time that will be done away with completely by God.

27) The Illumination will be like an ark, housing the faithful in the trust of God and keeping them moving forward, one step at a time towards their Father, until the flood of evil that is this world, declines and evaporates.

28) For believers, there must be preparation for the Illumination, too. Through the Sacraments, through the Beatitudes, the Church can fortify souls to be able to sustain the heat of God's loving glance upon the world. Every soul will need to proceed with caution and preparation, knowing the day will "transform" all, not just the lost sheep of Israel. All should trust in the goodness of the Lord, aware

that the faithful will now know Christ in a more intimate way. Never before has such a moment been realized. It will be beyond dreams—a bright day—like the morning after—at the Tomb.

29) Graces are provided for the Illumination. Graces never before seen have been and are being dispensed to all who are receptive to them. The critical juncture approaches, and God, in order to elicit appropriate responses, is paving the way for all hearts to return back to Him. We are at a confluence in time, in history, in the story of divine love—now to become better known. A divine family is about to be born on earth, as God comes to be with His children. Indeed, the Virgin Mary's Triumph has come, and it will be, as at Fatima, fulfilled through the power and glory of God—to again be visibly manifested in the sky, as at Fatima.

30) The light that will come into the world through the Illumination will especially benefit the family. This was foreshadowed at Fatima, when the Holy Family appeared in the sky on the last day of the apparitions in 1917. The great grace of the Illumination will heal and unite the family again, for God's rhythm and harmony in the world must begin with the family, and then spread throughout societies and civilization. As moths to a flame, the Illumination will draw families back together again. In the new times, God will dwell more closely with all His children, forming a divine family of love.

31) The Illumination will be a call from God to each person by *"name"*. By exposing the world and its false riches for what they are, mankind will move into a desert for a while, before grazing in the fertile and lush pastures of God's will on earth.

32)   With the Illumination comes the call for all to arise and crush the evil of the world. Satan's reign will be over, but the residue of his evil era will still need to be removed. The great miracle of conscience will be a calling to the soldiers of Christ, hidden from view now, to soon appear and to sever the remaining vestiges of the past. Which they will do, like a surgeon amputating a gangrened limb.

33)   The Commandments and the Beatitudes will provide an outline for God's orderly will in helping people to make the right choices after the Illumination. Even with a renewed conscience, the precarious times will be difficult and these aids, these guiding lights, will again serve as the path markers for all seeking to now right their lives, to turn to Christ in a sure and confident way.

34)   After the miracle, many will be able to hear God's voice in a new and special way. They will listen in their hearts, hearing their Father clearer and clearer as they continue down the path of purification, to perfection. It is to be a complementary process, the purer souls become, the clearer the voice of God will be in their hearts.

35)   After the Illumination, God's workers in the field will be obliged to provide God's children with answers, with the truth of what has happened to them. Like Father Phillip Bebie, who took the time to do so before his death, the faithful must be ready to help the return of the prodigals (**see Chapter 17**). Indeed, many will attempt to explain away the experience through rationalization or even lies. But because the great day of the Lord is to follow the Illumination, souls cannot be allowed, if possible, to slip back into their old ways. The truth of what occurred during the miracle will help many to hold the line, to continue in the world on the path of conversion until the purification

completes the process.

36)   The Era of Peace to come will be like a new covenant, a covenant of peace with God. Repentance and mercy will clear the way for all to make it home to their Father, Who, in the new times, needs to be known, loved and honored. The Father is ready and waiting to be presented to each of us. His peace will be the world's reward for returning to His waiting arms. In the distant future, His Feast Day in the Church will become the pinnacle day of the calender year.

37)   In the new era, the Illumination will have caused a new understanding of false doctrines and prophets. People will regret them, choosing the "truth of life" over the counterfeit doctrines of lies and death that this era has so thoroughly embraced.

38)   After the Illumination, Mary's presence will be even stronger, as she guides and protects God's lost sheep on their way back to the Lord. The Virgin will now take her position as the highly visible and beloved Queen of the new Kingdom.

39)   The Illumination of conscience will be like the cutting edge of truth slicing through the illusion that is this world. Those not prepared will have difficulty adjusting to the light which will penetrate powerfully into each soul. The Holy Spirit will move mightily in this effort, calling all souls to leave the era of sin and disobedience.

40)   The Illumination is an invitation to all who remain in the Lord or outside of the Lord. Those who reject the Illumination will be choosing to remain outside of Him, to be forever lost in the tempest that will sweep the world.

41) The Illumination will be the Lord's hand coming over the world, directing souls to Himself. As they respond, they will find themselves unburdened and transformed, ready to complete their journey back to God. Drinking deeply of God's heart and mind, they will thirst for more divine guidance and will seek the Lord's gifts. Some souls, who are like the walking dead now, who are like orphans—missing children of God—will be found and brought back to life. For the impossible is possible with God. Indeed, the miracle will be like a great current of love, sweeping souls into the ocean of God's mercy.

42) The Illumination will not reveal the truth of the Christian faith, but rather reawaken it, lifting a veil that has covered it; for God's truth has always been unchanging and immutable, although in our times, it has often been buried under misconceptions and false interpretations.

43) The Illumination will be like a trumpet calling God's own home in this time. Like in the Old Testament, a feast awaits at the end of the journey. All things are passing, only God is changeless, and those who respond will make merry at His table. Indeed, the horn will be sounded. The "warning" will be like the waving of God's banner, his standard—held higher than ever for all to see.

44) Time will be at its fullness when the Illumination strikes. God has outlined the approaching situation—an intersection of love filled with divine sustenance—in order to end an era of suffering and torment. It will be a gravitational process, a winnowing that will not only separate but illuminate the differences between the culture of life and the culture of death. Time now reopens, as we approach this moment, like a fig heavy on the bough. The drama has its actors and its audience, all prepared by God

for the great moment that will drive out all shadows, so the world will be bathed in light. Thus, it will finally be able to focus on its God, Who is to be revealed in glory.

45) The Illumination will redefine and recreate, out of the darkness and chaos of our times, the only true reality— which is God's truth. Mankind desires complication but with the great miracle of conscience, it will emerge from its deep sleep to God's simple truth. It will walk towards the light. It will call God by name, something He has wanted for a long time. This turning point is at hand, and the signs call it to our notice.

46) Held captive, oppressed, and mislead by the Evil One, the Illumination will allow mankind to see the pain it is experiencing from not knowing it's Father. Without our Father, there is only death, and this diagnosis will be arrived at by those living through the miracle. Indeed, the pages of our present life will be turned and new chapters will begin with the miracle. God will present Himself to mankind, to all His children as their Father. We will then only need to hand Him our fiat.

47) The Illumination will be a wake up call to all. But through faith, those who recognize the call will need to respond without delay. For in delaying to respond to what our conscience has been given, we would risk falling back into the shadows, locking out the light of God and the opportunity to embrace the Father's open hand.

48) Our response to the Illumination will be like a declaration of love for the Father, the Creator of all mankind. But God will not force His will upon anyone. Souls will have to want to come home. The defeat of evil in the world—so long in coming— will finally come. But not through violence—but through the

love of God's children for their Creator—after His voice resonates in their consciences. The Father is calling mankind to a liberty from sin. All souls need to stand ready, as an abrupt transition will take place for all to see and experience, followed by our need to choose. After which, during the purification, the Father will let loose on the world all that man continued to create and control in this century of ours, that was not of His will.

49) God views the Illumination as a time for mankind to turn to Him and to love, like flowers before the sun—who blossom at the exact moment, not a minute sooner or later. All that has led up to this time of the great miracle was also planned. The promise of Jesus Christ's divine and merciful intervention is about to be fulfilled, a part of God's plan from the beginning. Something, He has waited for with great expectation.

50) The story of the "Exodus" teaches us much about the coming miracle. As Moses parted the Red Sea by raising his arm, so will God now separate evil from good through the Illumination. After the miracle, those who listen to their conscience will pass through to the new era, free from the `bondage' of our sinful age. Those who don't will be eventually consumed by the purification. Likewise, God will expose to this generation, like he did with the Jews, it's love of idols and call upon us to turn away from them, especially the "great idol" of today — television (programing) and the cinema — which together ravages tens of millions of souls throughout the world. Finally, a sojourn in the "desert" can also be expected, as the full glory of the new era will not be capable of being immediately embraced without such an interim of time and trial. The Era of Peace is to be like the Land of Milk and Honey, but it may again take a generation or more to "fully" get there.

*

The Illumination will now bring answers to the ageless puzzle of the true meaning of the purpose of man, of creation. God will also now reveal the knowledge of His true paternity, which has been clouded and obscured by lies and deceit. What does it mean to be a child of God? Who is our Heavenly Father? The re-awakening is timely in measure, and true to the words in Scripture: **"Our Father, Who Art in Heaven, Hallowed by Thy name, Thy Kingdom Come, Thy Will Be Done on Earth as it is in Heaven."**

At Fatima, the promise of God's Triumph

CHAPTER SIXTEEN

THE POPE PREPARES THE CHURCH

"And in the four and twentieth day of the month the children of Israel came together with fasting and with sackcloth, and dust upon them. And the seed of the children of Israel seperated themselves from every stranger; and they stood, and confessed their sins, and the iniquities of their fathers."

— Neh 9:1-2

In 1917, the Blessed Virgin Mary promised at Fatima that an "Era of Peace" would be granted by God to the world. From Mary's words, we are given assurance that the world is not going to end in the immediate future, as some would believe, and that the new era, which denotes a specific epoch of time, will be especially filled with *"peace."*

Responding to the Bishop of Fatima's request, a commission of six experts appointed by the Bishop to interpret the message of Fatima rendered the opinion that the "Era of Peace" promised by Mary, implied a "true reign of Christ" on the earth. This was because, the commission stated, there could be no other meaning of the word "peace" on the lips of the Mother of Christ and no other meaning to her words "My Immaculate Heart will Triumph." This is not to confuse such a prophecy with millennial or millenarian theories that the Church has condemned—theories that embrace a literal thousand-year reign of Christ on earth or the belief that Christ will return at this time in history because of the new millennium. Properly understood, these prophecies of a new era are in line with

Pope John Paul II's vision of a new era, a new springtime in the Church, one which he has been directing the Church towards since the onset of his papacy.

This Second Pentecost, as the Holy Father has also called it, is to be a new beginning in the world for mankind. Ordained and directed by God the Father Himself, it is to be, as the Holy Father has written, a march toward salvation, centered on Christ, especially through His Eucharistic presence in the Church.

In order to prepare the Church for this era, an era the Pope understood to be appropriate in keeping with the 2,000 year anniversary of the birth of Jesus Christ, the Church prepared for four years to celebrate the Great Jubilee of the year 2000. The Jubilee, said the Pope, would mark the fullness of time, which recognizes that we are about to reach the end of a time in order to be prepared to consecrate a new beginning, a new time. Christ Himself, fulfilling the words of Isaiah (Is 61:1-2), marked such a period, a fullness of time when He read the passage out of Isaiah that spoke of the coming of the Messiah, and then said, "Today, this Scripture has been fulfilled in your hearing." Indeed, a new day had come, a new time had come, one anointed by the Holy Spirit and sent by the Father, and so it is to be again.

Preparing for the Great Jubilee, the Holy Father designated a period of four years from 1996 through 1999, as a period of preparation for the "new time." The first year, 1996, was especially designated as a year for a serious examination of conscience. The Pope wrote in his Apostolic Letter *Tertio Millenio Adveniente,* that Christians, "on the threshold of the new Millennium needed to place themselves humbly before the Lord and examine themselves on the responsibility which they too have for the evils of our day." There was a responsibility, he said, for the "grave forms of injustice and exclusion."

The following three years, 1997, 1998, and 1999 were dedicated to the Three Persons of the Holy Trinity, the Father, the Son, and the Holy Spirit, respectively. The thematic structure of this three year period, centered on Christ, the Son of God, made man. It was theological and, therefore, Trinitarian. Each of the three years were designed for Christians to have an opportunity to view their lives in accordance with the Gospels. Catholics were to seek the repentance, peace, and love of God, so readily available through Christ's power to change and heal lives, to embrace salvation, and to know the promise of eternal life in God.

Now that the Jubilee Year has dawned, the Pope continues with his efforts to right the wrongs of the past, to seek forgiveness and reconciliation, to clear the Church's conscience, and to lead the Church to a new beginning, a new springtime. Again, as occurred in 1996, the first year of the preparation, the Holy Father planned and then observed on March 12, 2000, in the spirit of the Lenten season, a special day of repentance and forgiveness. In a landmark public confession, Pope John Paul II begged God's forgiveness for the sins committed by Catholics over the past 2,000 years. The unprecedented moment of conscience was designed to continue the Pope's efforts to keep his vow of cleansing and reinvigorating Christianity for its third millennium. *"We forgive and ask forgiveness,"* the Holy Father said several times during a solemn Day of Pardon Mass in St. Peter's Basilica.

The conscience-clearing petition did not specifically mention the Church's every wrong, but clearly sought not to escape them, the most noticeable being the Crusades and the Inquisition: *"We are deeply saddened by the behavior of those who in the course of history have caused these children of yours to suffer and asking your forgiveness, we wish to commit ourselves to genuine brotherhood."* At the end of the confessions, Pope John Paul II embraced a large crucifix on the altar for the special Mass, imploring God's forgiveness. The following week, the Pope traveled to the Holy Land and continued to, once again, clear the conscience of the Church by acknowledging it's sins before the world. The Pope described his action as an attempt to "purify memory" of a sad history of hate, involving intolerance and omission.

For over three hundred years, and especially the last twenty, chosen souls have been foretelling the coming of the great miracle of conscience—an awakening of sorts—that will be the greatest miracle since the resurrection of Christ. This "mass enlightenment" will be a gift of grace to all mankind from God, they say, and it will somehow, most mysteriously, be received and felt to different degrees by every human being on earth. It will be an instantaneous epiphany of truth in the hearts and minds of all—a mini-judgement to a degree—and it will radically change the course of human history. For once experienced, much of mankind will begin a new quest for God, leaving behind its pursuit of the world. This new era will then reign until such depraved cravings arise again towards the end of the world, as believed by Christians will occur.

Is this moment of conscience illumination near? And if so, how should we prepare? The answer has been given to us by the Pope. Again, in light of his belief that a new epoch in the history of the Church is coming, a time of great enlightenment and reconciliation, a time of unity among Christians, the Pope's actions are perhaps reflective of what each and every Christian needs to do in the eyes and light of God in preparing for the new time, in preparing for God's great grace. While the Pope's "mea culpa" is offered on the behalf of all Catholics, it is time, he is telling the world, for each and every soul to examine their conscience and to personally seek forgiveness and renewal. We need to right our lives, to confess our sins now, to make reparation for our past mistakes. Indeed, just as the Pope has confronted the Church's mistakes of the past, we each, as individuals, need to do the same. We need to clean house, in order to be prepared for the awakening. It is an awakening, Fr. Phillip Bebie wrote long ago, that will be a taste of eternity—a sign of the future—a moment like no other.

Before he died, Father Bebie wrote about the illumination of conscience as if it had already taken place and the faithful were now in need of an understanding of what they had just experienced. Excerpted from his book, *The Warning*, Fr. Bebie's words serve as a perfect summary to our understanding and preparation for the great approaching day of the illumination of all consciences.

"We forgive and ask forgiveness."

-Pope John Paul II
March 12, 2000

"The Warning is the first step for the conversion of the world."

-Fr. Philip Bebie

Fr. Philip Bebie

CHAPTER SEVENTEEN

AFTER THE WARNING
BY FR. PHILIP BEBIE

"As the years of a tree, so the years of my people; and my chosen ones shall long enjoy the produce of their hands. They shall not toil in vain, nor beget children for sudden destruction; For a race blessed by the Lord are they and their offspring."

— Is 65: 22-23

We have just experienced The Warning (the illumination of all consciences). The Warning was like the conversion of Saint Paul the Apostle, who was penetrated by the same light we have recently endured. He was on the Damascus road, journeying to that town to persecute. In a glorious vision it was revealed to him that he was assailing not only the members of the Church, but Jesus Himself, the very Lord of heaven and earth! The blinding light of the Risen Christ convicted him of sin. Paul heeded the warning Jesus had given him; he repented and became his faithful follower, and left his former life behind.

Has not the same enlightenment been accorded to us all in The Warning? The grace once granted to an individual has finally penetrated every human heart in a single, sudden burst of divine light. We have felt the same grace, the same light, that Paul did. God would have the whole world respond just as Paul did. We must now repent of the sin the Lord has shown us in ourselves by

The Warning, and amend our lives, following Jesus.

The Warning made us aware of God. Everyone, unbeliever as well as believer, now can declare that God has touched us with His immeasurable power. He has intervened in an unprecedented manner to make all people aware of His existence, His mercy, His sovereign rulership, His love for us and His concern for our salvation. There is a God, and he is good. No one can now any longer deny Him unless he chooses to fling the truth back in God's face. The Warning has made God evident. We have felt His power in our bones.

The Warning shows us our sins. It was predicted as a "correction of the conscience of the world." The Scripture foretold long ago that Jesus would send the Holy Spirit to "convict the world of sin." If we did not fully understand before what that meant, we do now, by the power of the Warning. Sin, our resistance to becoming the loving kind of person God is, results in many unloving deeds, decisions, and attitudes. These were all vividly clear in the brilliant light God shone in our souls. Our consciences were thoroughly illuminated at that moment, exposing all the self-deception we are so clever at, pulling out the dead memories that have never been leavened with love, uncovering the lies we told ourselves, the compromises we made. We saw so blatantly the many harsh, stubborn, and unkind decisions we have made, the times we cruelly trod on the feelings of other people, coveted their possessions, envied their good fortune and rejoiced at their failures. Then we groaned with anguish when God revealed to us the neglect, the refusal to help, the undone deeds and the unfulfilled plans. We have heard Him say to us, "Why have you persecuted Me?"

The Warning was a taste of eternity. Time stopped for a moment during The Warning, and the truth of timeless existence tumbled in on all of us. It was no longer possible, because of The Warning, to hide from ourselves. All we ever did was before our eyes, seen all at once, in a single glance. We knew then how God's gaze crosses all barriers and grasps the uttermost secrets. He shared with us, for our conversion, how He sees us, and we beheld, in an instant mercifully brief, whatever in us was displeasing to Him. What we understood was our eternal state, shoulder we have died at that time. We suffered for a moment the pain of our sin, the pain of separation from God, the pain of Purgatory or Hell. God let us see it all, in The Warning.

The Warning was a mercy from God. By The Warning we became aware that we are not yet what He wants us to be. We felt the pain of being unlike Him, far from Him. His will is for us to become like Himself, happy in all that He is, and to become close to Him. Sin is the only impediment to that. It prevents us from achieving perfect, even eternal happiness. God unveiled our sinfulness to us in The Warning, not out of revenge, for vengefulness is foreign to His heart, but rather out of love and mercy. He wants us to never have to suffer again the pain we felt in The Warning. His mercy allowed us to sample the pain that sin bequeaths to us. The Warning was truly a mercy from God.

The Warning is a sign of the future. It is the major turning-point in world history, the most important "sign of the times." The Warning tells us that all has gone before in the entire course of world history now focuses on the years just ahead of us. Our age is absolutely critical for the salvation of the human race. A large proportion of all the people who have ever lived are actually living on earth right now. They must have the opportunity to hear and know of God's plan of salvation for them. They need to learn that Jesus has come to take away their sins. All must understand that sin alone deprives us of happiness and the glory of God. Sin is our only real enemy, the only adversary that can destroy us forever. The Warning has prepared all the world's people for the message of the Gospel, prepared them all for Jesus and His life. By The Warning we all know of our sin. We know we need a Savior. The Warning is the first step for the conversion of the entire world. Without knowing our own sin, we would never understand how much we need Jesus and His forgiveness.

The Warning is a direct intervention from God. Never before has God acted directly and universally to make everyone in the world completely aware of their sinfulness before His holiness. The preaching of the Gospel through the witness of the Church has been available for centuries, so it is not as if He had never made such a revelation of this kind before. But it has not happened in history before that He has acted with such power, such precision, such instance. The time must be very special. There must not be much time left for repentance. As a race we have repudiated the Gospel message so often and responded to is so sluggishly that what God meant the world to be, in peace, never came to be. The constant pleading of Mary for us to turn back to God, and her remonstrances over the years while we listened not, are, for believers, sufficient evidence that the present age is even worse than earlier ones. But time is running out. "The times" are about to end, and a new age of peace is promised. The Warning is the first dramatic sign to all that the old age is ending. It is not God's wish that we be among those who refused to repent in time. Not in all the ages is it ever His wish that even a single one of His little ones be lost. For this reason He has intervened, so that the danger would be manifest, the evil of the present day unmasked and the darkness of false "enlightenment" be exposed. If the world has not wanted to listen to the truth, and the Father's little ones are being misled, He, in His sovereign majesty and power, will compel it to listen. With The Warning. He sweeps away all the sophistry and deception with which Satan has obscured the light of the Gospel.

The Warning calls us to choose. We know now, by the grace of The Warning, that each of us has a fateful choice to make. We can choose either to flee from our sin or remain in it. Despite the power of The Warning, we still have our freedom to choose—we posses a free will. If God took that away from us, we would no longer be human, able to love or to refrain from loving. We have the ability to say "Yes" or "No," and The Warning confronts us with that responsibility. There is no middle ground. The only choice we have is to be for God or against Him. The situation is just as it was on Mount Carmel, when Elijah called God's people to stand with him and the Lord or with the prophets of Baal and Ashteroth. Like them, we have a choice; choose God, or no-gods; life, or death.

The Warning has made it impossible to delay a decision any longer. To delay is itself a choice for sin. To obtain everlasting life with God we have to amend our lives as disciples of the Lord Jesus, who alone knows the way to the Father. The alternative is to be lost forever in the pain we fleetingly felt when we knew The Warning. Bliss, or agony—Heaven or Hell—that is the dilemma. Everything for us depends on which path we select for ourselves!

"Souls, buried in darkness, buried in years of serious sin, are going to be saved through the mercy of this miracle."

The miracle will reflect God the Father's glory and power.

EPILOGUE

WAVES OF POWER AND PAIN

"Repent, therefore, and be converted, that your sins may be wiped away, and that the Lord may grant you times of refreshment and send you the Messiah already appointed for you, Jesus, whom Heaven must receive until the times of universal restoration of which God spoke through the mouth of his holy prophets from of old."

— Acts 3:19-21

Though the miracle of conscience foretold to soon come has been adequately described by visionaries, perhaps the emphasis of these accounts is too subjective, too attached to the exact words given to them by their heavenly sources. We especially see this in their acknowledgment that some "fear" and "pain" are to be expected in regards to the unfolding of this event.

These accounts are true, but the miracle must be understood for what it will truly be: a great gift of grace emanating from the heart of God to the hearts of His children! Thus, while this event may strike fear and pain in the hearts of people, for the most part, these uncomfortable feelings will quickly melt from the intensity of God's love once souls understand their discomfort is coming from the love and mercy of their God.

In Scripture, we find examples of this understanding. In Genesis, we read how Adam and Eve became afraid when they heard God calling them in the Garden. Moses, too, hid his face in fear, after first hearing the Lord speak to him from the burning bush. Hundreds of years later, at the Annunciation, the most chosen soul of all-time is alleviated of her fear by the Angel Gabriel, who comes to her with God's words of comfort and assurance. Likewise, St. Paul, on the road to Damascus, trembled in the Lord's presence. These souls, five of the most chosen in Judeo-Christian history, could not help but cower and sense alarm as they were bathed in the light of God.

Over the centuries, we find more accounts of visionaries and chosen souls who were cautioned not to fear, not be afraid of their "annunciation." Like Scripture's great ones, the uneasiness these souls exhibited was a rightful apprehension, considering the uniqueness of their circumstances. But all were put at ease once they knew what was happening to them was of God, of His ways, which though uncomfortable, are never harmful. Theologians say that the responses of these souls must be understood as the only way any soul would feel in the presence of such grace, no matter how blessed and pure, as noted in the Virgin Mary's reaction to Gabriel.

Therefore, the coming illumination of all consciences needs to be seen in this same light. It is to be the world's "annunciation," and in lieu of the suspicion that so many souls at this time are said to be in a state of serious sin, the fact that this event has been prophesied to shake up people, to cause them pain, can even be understood as being logical, considering how God created us to be pure and holy, like Him. Like the Prodigal Son, whose conscience was struck by guilt and shame, and who agonized in his thoughts as he returned to his father's home, our hearts and minds will be shaken too during the illumination of our souls. But God has always allowed pain for growth and conversion, a small price to pay versus the sufferings of the eternal loss of one's soul.

Moreover, the great miracle to come must be understood in even a more profound way. A great, penetrating light from God will not just be shone on earth in the form of an extraordinary blessing, as often described. Rather, God Himself, as He did in Scripture with Adam and Eve, Moses, the Virgin Mary, and St. Paul, will be moving towards His people in a powerful, unprecedented way. And this intimate nearness, this closeness of the divine, will make us feel, the way they felt. During the illumination, we are going to be in the presence of God in a new and special way for a brief period of time, and our soul's response, be that what it may, will be appropriate, considering the "power" of divine love.

God, with His mighty, protective arms, is coming to hold His children and they will feel His strength, His protective power through this event. But this will be good for souls, and the world, for the time is ripe for such a moment, or God would not have ordained it. The Father's will for His people during the illumination will be experienced with justice and mercy, for He desires to save each and every soul, and will use "His ways" to accomplish "His mission."

On the day of the illumination, each soul will have to listen to their heart, for the moment will be, like the crashing of waves, the pounding of the sea, a time of reckoning for mankind. In essence, it will be a reunion with its Father. Through the illumination of consciences, the Eternal Father is coming to tell His children that they have been away for a long time, too long, and that He is calling them back, not to punish them, but to rescue them. This is part of the plan God envisioned from the beginning for this time in history. But the season for the Father's reunion with His children is upon us and there will be no turning back.

God in essence, is coming at this time, in this powerful way, to save the world, to save the many souls who, because of the darkness of our sinful times, would be destined for Hell. Indeed, God is aware of the great destruction of lives and souls Satan has caused, often unfairly in this century. This is true especially now, as all moral sanity has collapsed. Through the Evil One's snares, countless souls are now in serious trouble, perhaps headed for Hell. But now, with the greatest act of divine mercy, God is going to pull the rug out from under the devil's feet at the last second, just when the Evil One has gained control of almost all of mankind. Souls, buried in darkness, buried in years of serious sin, are going to be saved through the mercy of this miracle. God, at the critical moment, is going to offset centuries of Satan's work, thus preventing the devil from reaping the harvest of souls he has worked so hard for, especially in our dark times—times when sin has become justified, legalized and glorified.

In light of all of the suffering and death that has transpired over the centuries, especially the bloody, genocide-filled 20th century, the coming illumination will eventually be understood as the "true" beginning of the era of peace promised at Fatima. In mankind's turn towards it's Creator through this great event, the promises of our forefathers are fulfilled, and all those children presently outside of the will of the Father are being invited, through His extraordinary love and His indomitable power, back into the rhythm and harmony of His will. Thus, all things have been put into place for this moment in time and all God's children, like the Prodigal Son, are being welcomed home, regardless of their past. Visionaries say that time is turning back upon itself, as the Holy Spirit is said to be desiring to rush forward to its ultimate end—the restoration of all of God's children on earth to there Heavenly Father.

In the final period to now come, whole nations will convert to the Church, as well as whole peoples. The Protestants, the Moslems, and eventually the Jews—through the power of God—are going to find unity with their separated brethren. The impossible, like never before, will be shown to be possible, for as Scripture says, nothing is impossible for God. This coming miracle then will be a surge of power, designed to overcome the tremendous effects of generations of sin and error. Indeed, power and pain, both in waves, are coming with this event. After which, the last chapter of man's history will be written.

"So do not pass premature judgment before the Lord comes, who will bring to light things hidden by darkness and will reveal the inner motives. Then will each one experience his approval from God."

- 1 Cor 4:5

"Concern yourself with My coming, for I come 'soon' to be among My children in a new way, unforseen by man but foretold by your Mother."
-The Eternal Father to Barbara Centilli
February 22, 2000

The Virgin Mary

NOTES

INTRODUCTION

Fr. Federico Suarez's quote is from his book, *The Afterlife; Death, Judgment, Heaven and Hell.*

CHAPTER ONE
THE FUNCTION OF CONSCIENCE

Most of the information on conscience formation came from the books, *Hell,* by Fr. Schouppe, S.J. and *How To Avoid Hell*, by Thomas Nelson (Tan Books). I also referenced, among others, Fr. Garrigou Lagrange's book *Everlasting Life* (Tan Books) and *Preparation For Death* (Tan Books) by St. Alphonsus Liguori.

CHAPTER TWO
THE PARTICULAR JUDGMENT

The information on the Particular Judgment came primarily from Fr. Lagrange's *Everlasting Life* and St. Alphonsus Liguori's *Preparation For Death.*

CHAPTER THREE
THE GENERAL JUDGMENT

The information on the General Judgment came primarily from Fr. Lagrange's *Everlasting Life* and St. Alphonsus Liguori's

Preparation For Death. I also referenced the author's own book, *The Fatima Prophecies,* for the information on Fatima.

CHAPTER FOUR
THE MIRACLE OF THE ILLUMINATION OF ALL CONSCIENCES

The information contained in this chapter is from the author's research on many books and articles over the last two decades. Some of it was taken directly from the author's 1995 book, *Call of the Ages.*

CHAPTER FIVE
THE PROPHECIES

The prophecies in this chapter were taken from many sources, primarily from *Call of the Ages,* by the author.

CHAPTER SIX
GARABANDAL

The story of the apparitions and prophecies of Garabandal were excerpted, once again, from the author's book, *Call of the Ages.* The Bishop of Santander's letter was published by various Marian organizations in 1996. Father Bebie's comments were taken from his book, *The Warning.*

CHAPTER SEVEN
CONTEMPORARY REVELATIONS

The revelations published in this chapter were excerpted from the author's book, *Call of the Ages.*

CHAPTER EIGHT
BARBARA CENTILLI

The revelations of Barbara Centilli came from *Seeing With the Eyes of the Soul (Vol's I, II, and III)*, published by St. Andrews Productions, 6111 Steubenville Pike, McKees Rocks, PA, 15136.

CHAPTER NINE
FR. STEFANO GOBBI

Fr. Stefano Gobbi's messages were excerpted from his book, *Our Lady Speaks to Her Beloved Son,* published by the Marian Movement of Priests, USA chapter.

CHAPTER TEN
MATTHEW KELLY

The story of Matthew Kelly and his message were excerpted from the author's book, *The Fatima Prophecies.* The message on the Mini-Judgment itself can also be found in Kelly's book *Words from God.*

CHAPTER ELEVEN
A PREVIEW OF THE ILLUMINATION:
SOULS WHO HAVE EXPERIENCED JUDGMENT

The story of the souls who have experienced an illumination is from the author's book, *Call of the Ages.*

CHAPTER TWELVE
FR STEPHEN SCHEIER

The account of Fr. Stephen Scheier's judgment comes from the author's personal meetings with Fr. Scheier and from hearing him speak. I also quoted Fr. Scheier from the highly recommended video, *Prophecies And The New Times*, by MaxKoll Productions.

CHAPTER THIRTEEN
CHRISTOPHER WINTERS

The account of Christopher Winters's judgement experience was taken from the author's personal interview and correspondence with Mr. Winters.

CHAPTER FOURTEEN
DR. FRANK NOVASACK

The account of Dr. Frank Novasack Jr.'s judgement "dream" was taken from the author's personal interview and correspondence with Dr. Novasack.

CHAPTER FIFTEEN
A DEEPER UNDERSTANDING

The author's own research, along with his own interpretations of many revelations, went into the writing of this chapter.

CHAPTER SIXTEEN
THE POPE PREPARES THE CHURCH

The information on Fatima in this chapter came from the author's book, *The Fatima Prophecies*. Pope John Paul II's Apostolic letter, *Tertio Millennio Adveniente* was published in December, 1994. His published confessions in the year 2000 were carried by all the major Catholic publications.

CHAPTER SEVENTEEN
AFTER THE WARNING

"After the Warning" by Father Philip Bebie was excerpted from his book, *The Warning*.

EPILOGUE
WAVES OF POWER AND PAIN

The author wrote this chapter from his own interpretations and studies of the prophesied miracle.

SELECTED BIBLIOGRAPHY

Albright, Judith M. *Our Lady at Garabandal*. Milford, Ohio: Faith Publishing Company, 1992.

Bebie, Father Philip C.P. *The Warning*. Asbury, New Jersey: 101 Foundation, 1986.

Brown, Michael H. *The Final Hour*. Milford, Ohio: Faith Publishing Company, 1992.

Centilli, Barbara. *Seeing with the Eyes of the Soul*. (Vols I-III) McKees Rocks, Pennsylvania: St. Andrew's Productions, 1998, 1999, 2000.

Chandier, Russell. *Doomsday*. Ann Arbor, Michigan: Servant Publications, 1993.

Flynn, Ted. *Prophecies and the New Times*. (Video) Sterling, Virginia: MaxKol Institute, 1997.

Flynn, Ted and Maureen. *The Thunder of Justice*. Sterling, Virginia: MaxKol Communications, Inc., 1993.

Francois, Robert. *O Children Listen to Me*. Lindenhurst, New York: The Workers of Our Lady of Mount Carmel. Inc., 1980.

Garcia, Veronica. *Messages of Love*. Veronica Garcia, 1992.

Gobbi, Don Stefano. *Our Lady Speaks to Her Beloved Sons*. St.

Francis, Maine: National Headquarters of the Marian Movement of Priests in the United States of America, 1988.

Haffert, John M. *The Great Event*. Asbury, New Jersey: The 101 Foundation, Inc., 2000.

Kelly, Matthew. *Words From God*. Batesman Bay, N.S.W. Australia, 1993.

Kowalska, Sister M. Faustina. *Divine Mercy in My Soul*. (The Diary of Sister M. Faustina Kowalska) Stockbridge, Massachusetts: Marian Press, 1987.

Laffineur, Fr. Matiene and M.T. le Pelletier. *Star on the Mountain*. Lindenhurst, New York: Our Lady of Mount Carmel de Garabandal, Inc., 1969.

Lagrange, Garrigou Fr. Reginald. O.P. *Everlasting Life*. Rockford, Illinois: TAN books and Publishers, Inc., 1991.

Liguori. St. Alphonsus. *Preparation for Death*. Rockford, Illinois: TAN books and Publishers, Inc., 1982.

Nelson, Thomas A. *How To Avoid Hell*. Rockford, Illinois: TAN books and Publishers, Inc., 1989.

Paul II, Pope John. "Tertio Millenio Adveniente" in *Inside the Vatican*. New Hope, Kentucky: St. Martin de Porres Lay Dominican Community Print Shop, December, 1994.

Pelletier, Joseph A., A.A. *God Speaks at Garabandal*. Worcester, Massuchusetts: Joseph A. Pelletier, A.A., 1970.

Perez, Ramon. *Garabandal - The Village Speaks*. Lindenhurst, New York: The Workers of Our Lady of Mount Carmel, Inc., 1981.

Petrisko, Thomas W. *Call of the Ages.* Santa Barbara, California: Queenship Publishing Inc., 1995.

Petrisko, Thomas W. *Inside Heaven and Hell.* McKees Rocks, Pennsylvania: St. Andrews Productions, 2000.

Petrisko, Thomas W. *Inside Purgatory.* McKees Rocks, Pennsylvania: St. Andrews Productions, 2000.

Petrisko, Thomas W. *The Last Crusade.* McKees Rocks, Pennsylvania: St. Andrews Productions, 1997.

Petrisko, Thomas W. *The Kingdom of Our Father.* McKees Rocks, Pennsylvania: St. Andrews Productions, 1999.

Petrisko, Thomas W. (Editor) *Our Lady Queen of Peace - Special Edition I.* Pittsburgh Center for Peace, 1991.

Petrisko, Thomas W. *The Fatima Prophecies: At the Doorstep of the World.* McKees Rocks, Pennsylvania: St. Andrews Productions, 1998.

Ross, Gerald G. *More Personal Revelations of Our Lady of Light.* Fort Mitchell, Kentucky: Our Lady of Light Publications, 1992.

Schouppe, Fr. S.J. *Hell.* Rockford, Illinois: TAN Books and Publishers, Inc., 1989.

Suarez, Federico. *The Afterlife, Death, Judgement., Heaven and Hell.* Manila, Phillipines: Sinag-tala Publishers, Inc., 1986 (English translation).

Williams, Fr. David. *A Textual Concordance of the Holy Scriptures.* Rockford, Illinois: TAN Books and Publishers, Inc, 1985.

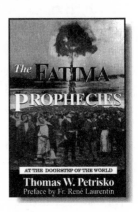
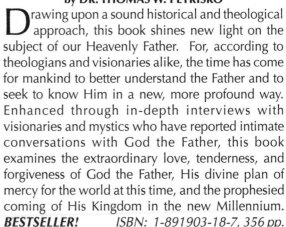

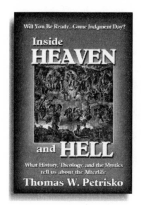
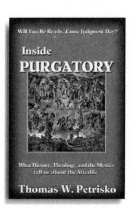

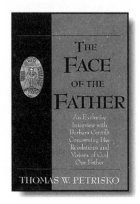
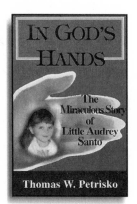